PRAISE FOR SWEATING BULLETS

"Congratulations on this excellent book to help business people with speaking to audiences. The dialogue format of telling a story to disarm the reader who can benefit from this guidance is brilliant. I find that effective communication skills rank as the top priority for leaders of organizations. Great communicators can be great leaders. Poor communicators will run into a wall they cannot overcome without help. Your book provides that help."

Dennis L. Johnson, President & Chief Executive Officer, United Heritage Mutual Holding Company, United Heritage Financial Group, United Heritage Life Insurance Company

"Dale has been instrumental in working with our communications team and executive leadership team in sharpening our messaging and presentation skills. Sweating Bullets is an engaging, quick read that puts Dale's expertise in your hands with an action packed plan that includes effective practical tips to overcome anxiety and deliver a meaningful message."

Virginia Aulin, VP, Human Resources, Communications and Corporate Affairs, Packaging Corporation of America

"In *Sweating Bullets*, Dale shares a clear, actionable pathway to significantly improving your presenting skills. By combining practical ideas with a sharp focus on the purity of purpose, Dale opens up several gems for anyone to increase the impact of their presentations."

Ron Price, Price-Associates and author of
Treasure Inside* and *The Complete Leader

"As Chloe did for Mack, Dale has given us a wonderful gift in the form of this story, laying out lessons learned and giving us the tools we need to hone our presentation and communication skills."

Lynn McConnell, Director, Human Resources, Hawley Troxell

"I've known Dale Dixon for years and have heard him present numerous times. He is always able to capture the attention of his audience and make the experience memorable. Beginner or seasoned veteran, you'll be inspired and have new tools to engage your audiences. Dale offers invaluable lessons on being a powerful presenter and communicator. As a small business owner and content expert who regularly speaks to many audiences, I highly recommend and encourage you read this for your own well-being!"

Rhea Allen, President/CEO Peppershock Media and
Integrative Marketing Consultant

"At the outset, I could not imagine that this book would actually have relevance for me. I know I "present" every day, one way or the other, but the initial reaction to the word "presentation" pushed me into the camp of thinking this book was about someone else. I'm not a presenter. The biggest surprise was to find that this was about me, indeed."

Dr. Ken Swaim, Swaim Chiropractic

"The story was engaging and informative. It definitely got the point across that even those who do not have confidence in their presenting skills can become impactful presenters with guidance and practice, and those who are confident presenters always have much more to learn and improve on."

Donna Price Shines, Executive Director/CEO,
The Mentoring Network, Inc.

"I was engaged, the lessons were clear, and it was an easy read. It is refreshing to see an author use clear language. Much more effective than a dry textbook. "

Dan Whiting, Federal Strategist, ADG Creative

"It is fabulous. I found myself using the lessons as I worked to prepare a training for our department. It is very easy to follow; the personal story makes it more engaging and relatable. Great lessons, clear points."

Brenda Maynard Walters, Senior Immigration Administrator

"Dale provides an excellent book that many public speakers can relate to. His years of experience benefit the reader with genuine opportunities to see themselves in the examples given. I recommend Sweating Bullets for anyone wanting to improve their presentation skills."

LeRoy Forsman, Chief of Police (Retired),
Author of *Live Like a Leader 24/7*

SWEATING BULLETS

A Story About Overcoming the Fear of Public Speaking

DALE DIXON

Sweating Bullets: A Story About Overcoming the Fear of Public Speaking
By Dale Dixon

For further information about speaking engagements, professional consultation, special bulk pricing, or other related inquiries, see the author's website at daledixonmedia.com.

Cover Design: Cari Campbell, Cari Campbell Design
Interior Design: Fusion Creative Works
Primary Editor: Kim Foster
Project Manager: Hannah Cross

Print ISBN: 978-1-61206-080-4
eBook ISBN: 978-1-61206-081-1
Library of Congress Control Number: 2013950700

Published by Aloha Publishing
www.AlohaPublishing.com

Second Printing
Printed in the United States of America

To my best friend, confidant, cheerleader, and anchor, my wife.
Tonia, I love you more than words can describe.

TABLE OF CONTENTS

INTRODUCTION

I was sitting at the anchor desk of a local TV station. I remember it vividly. I had an epiphany. After several years of anchoring the news and reporting more stories than I could remember, it hit me: "All I have to do is be me."

Looking back on the moment, it seems so simple. As with so many simple things in life, the lesson is profound. Each evening, before each newscast, I would get myself worked up, nervous, and anxious. Why? I was speaking in front of a crowd of people. Yes, those people were in living rooms, and we were connected via video cameras, broadcast equipment, a transmitter, and televisions, but it was Communication 101. I was telling a story and it didn't matter if it was one, one hundred, one thousand, ten thousand, or one hundred thousand people watching. I had to perform.

At the heart of the epiphany was the realization that I have what it takes. If I can talk to one person, face-to-face; I can talk to one hundred thousand. Effectively communicating with one person is just as important as effectively communicating with one hundred thousand.

I'm here to tell you, "You have what it takes." Think about your life. Each day, you are in contact with countless people. You interact with a few face to face, having in-depth conversations. Some inter-actions will be once-in-a-lifetime opportunities—a job interview or big sales presentation. Others will be the quickly forgotten chance meeting—the chatty clerk at an out-of-town grocery store during a trip or a conversation with a stranger on the ski chairlift.

Then, there's the mundane. It shouldn't be mundane, but human nature dictates that repetition becomes routine and loses its luster. Conversations with your spouse, family, friends, coworkers, and col-leagues rarely receive a second thought. The interaction is natural. You're simply communicating.

In the midst of all of these interactions is the peripheral: people within earshot who watch your actions and listen to your words.

It might be a paradigm-shifting thought, but your life really is a pre-sentation. You are constantly communicating a message. Most of the time, you don't give it a second thought.

In light of your day-to-day presenting, why is it that giving a formal presentation causes so much anxiety? Yes, the stakes are higher, but you have so much practice presenting. What if you could find confi-dence in the amount of presentation practice you possess?

So often, people facing the high-stakes presentation lose sight of the communication skill they possess. That's why I wrote *Sweating Bullets* as a story. Actually, the following pages contain a fable. I thought it important to use the structure of a story to convey pow-erful lessons to help you turn the daily practice of communication into the confidence to effectively present a high-stakes message.

Those I've helped with their presentation skills didn't immediately realize their inherent expertise in communication. Effectively com-municating a message is the same process, whether it's with a friend, family member, or a stranger at the grocery store. It could involve two people on a sales call, ten people in a boardroom, or a hundred people in an audience at a convention hall. The stakes may be much higher for the larger audience, but they are people, nonetheless, and the art of sharing information remains the same.

Join me on a journey of mixing historical fact with fiction as I share some real-life experiences through fictionalized characters in an attempt to help you become a better presenter.

THE POWER OF A STORY

Remember hearing a story that stirred an emotion? Do your favorite songs remind you of a joyful (or painful) time in your life? Start paying attention to your surroundings, and you'll see and hear so many stories. Your favorite song probably tells a story. The advertisement that catches your attention probably tells a story. People with whom you enjoy interacting probably have a good story to tell.

Stories contain the most effective means to convey a message. We experienced the power of stories as children. Why is it, then, that we migrate away from stories in high school and college, attempting to learn through lecture, statistics, facts, and figures? Sure, there's a place for those things. But what is most memorable? The story.

WHAT YOU CAN EXPECT FROM THIS STORY

Mack Thompson is an executive plagued with self-doubt about his ability to speak in front of a crowd of people. His level of discomfort in front of an audience makes me squirm, and perhaps it will do the same to you.

Mack has a chance meeting with a skilled presenter, Chloe Parker. He takes the bold step of asking Chloe to teach him a thing or two about presenting. Each chapter will give you a glimpse at how Mack and Chloe work through the typical stumbling blocks we all experience as communicators.

At the end of each chapter, you'll see a **Bullet Points** section. Here, you will receive additional resources to seek out and dive a little deeper into specific, presentation-related issues.

Throughout the book are the **Seven Laws of Presenting**. Each is a bite-sized nugget to keep you focused on what really matters as you work to improve your communication skills.

My sincere desire is that Mack's story will inspire you to consider the communication skill and talent within you. They just need a little coaxing and coaching to be released.

1

MACK'S NIGHTMARE

"You may not realize it when it happens, but a kick in the teeth may be the best thing in the world for you."
—*Walt Disney*

A small bead of sweat began to form just above Mack's hairline. He could feel it start to trickle down his scalp, and it added to the list of unconscious and uncontrolled reactions his body was having.

Oxygen was escaping him. The muscles around his throat kept tightening like a vice. He looked down to see a tightening grip on the inclined laminate board that created the top of the lectern as he tried to steady himself against buckling knees. Mack knew if he loosened his hands, they would start trembling. Each breath was shallow. He could only gasp for a moment and could feel a small bit of air enter the upper part of his lungs. He looked up. The massive room, in which he was the focal point, was a blur.

"Uh, let me figure this out," Mack stammered. About a thousand people were watching Mack's self-implosion. Sitting ten to a table, the crowd was part of the Chamber of Commerce's annual economic forum. As Chief Operating Officer of InCirq, Inc., a tech company in Boise, Idaho, Mack had earned respect from most in the audience simply by his title. InCirq was one of the top three computer chip makers in the world.

"You know," Mack paused, looking over his left shoulder, then his right. He was obviously trying to catch a glimpse of the two massive video screens situated on either side of the wall behind him. "Um…" The PowerPoint slides on those screens looked foreign to Mack. His reaction told the audience he didn't have a clue what should be on the screen. "Let's take a look at the next slide," Mack said. Silence. The slide didn't advance. "Wasn't someone in charge of advancing the slides?" Mack thought to himself. Embarrassment mixed with frustration, along with a dose of desperation, forced the COO to try to take some measure of control.

"Um…" Seconds felt like minutes as Mack worked to gain his composure and deliver some semblance of the message he had been asked to present on behalf of his company. Previous speakers hadn't been that incredible as they dryly explained the economic downturn and slow-but-sure rebound. Mack's mind was working to rationalize his performance by comparing it to those before him.

Norman Reynolds sat at table nine in the center of the room. Norman's position on the InCirq board was a source of pride in retirement. He'd worked in the tech industry beginning in the days when computers occupied entire rooms. Norman leaned toward the man sitting to his right, whom he didn't know, and said with smirk, "You know, this Mack guy better not quit his day job. He needs to stay in his office back at headquarters." Norman leaned back in his chair with a satisfied grin, not waiting for a response.

"Um…" The blur continued for Mack. The room continued to be a fog of nondescript faces. Words coming out of Mack's mouth became an unmemorable monotone stream, forced words interrupted by a methodical, constant "um" and an awkward pause for the PowerPoint slide transition.

Mack was coming off a three-week intense travel schedule. His extent of preparation for the economic forum speech amounted to an e-mailed list of bullet points to his assistant, Mary, with instructions to, "Throw a PowerPoint together. Here's what I want to talk about." He remembered hitting send on that e-mail two weeks ago, then not making time for his mind to prepare for the moments that were now causing so much pain.

He had rationalized the lack of planning. He knew the material. For crying out loud, he was the COO. He was busy. This was just another meeting. Nobody would be paying attention. The realization flooded over him. This was not just another meeting. One thousand people, who would remember, were watching him.

Finally, Mack felt he was at a place where he could draw a conclusion and sit down. He wished he could simply walk off the stage, find the nearest exit, and escape back to his office. He knew that wasn't an option.

A large tabletop placard with "Mack Thompson" written on it sat in front of an empty seat at the head table, which flanked the podium where Mack had just felt so much pain. Mack finished, "Um, thank you for your time." He turned just in time for one more awkward moment. Mack hadn't noticed the emcee was standing beside him and now was directly between him and his seat. Mack hadn't taken the time to get to know the person, not thinking it important. After all the embarrassment, human nature took over and Mack didn't want to look anyone in the eye, so he shuffled left just as the emcee took a confident step right. Then, Mack shuffled right as the emcee reached out his left hand to grab Mack's right elbow, pulling his forearm forward into a quick handshake. The action felt like a freeing catapult away from the situation. Mack slid into his seat and grabbed for the glass of water sitting next to his name card. Now, Mack took a deep breath, mostly in relief. The next speaker took the podium, and Mack immediately noticed her confidence.

SWEATING BULLETS

At thirty-five, Chloe Parker had gotten her start in the tech world, working in marketing for a few start-ups. She and a group of friends had begun developing apps in the off-hours as a way to make money and learn the ins and outs of development. The group had made a name for itself in the local community because of its loosely formed nature and success in developing unique apps for small businesses.

"Let me tell you how not to build an app," Chloe started her presentation to the chamber crowd.

Immediately, Chloe captured Mack's attention. He noticed a dramatic change in the room. There had been a dull murmur of whispers and movement in the audience, everything from people shifting in seats to milling about in the back of the room. Chloe's first ten words stopped the low-level noise that had been present through Mack's entire presentation.

Chloe didn't use PowerPoint. She told stories about herself and the group of designers with whom she worked and shared the successes of some of the small companies that had employed the group to do the work of building apps.

By the time Chloe finished, Mack had learned things about the growing app-building business he had no idea existed in this relatively small town.

Before he knew it, Mack was hearing Chloe conclude her remarks. "Yes, there's an app for that," she said. "And if there isn't, most importantly, there's someone within twenty miles of you who has the expertise to build the app you need. It doesn't need to be the group of people I work with, but I encourage you to start local when you start shopping for a developer. A wealth of talent is ready to work for you."

Sincere applause erupted throughout the auditorium. It wasn't the obligatory smattering of polite hand clapping Mack had heard at the end of his presentation.

BULLET POINTS

The feeling of failure tends to remain imprinted on the mind. A poor presentation can nag at your subconscious for weeks, months—maybe years. The question is: what are you going to do about it?

Even though Mack was feeling the pain of an embarrassing performance, he took notice of Chloe's presentation. He wasn't quite sure what he was seeing, but he was aware of his surroundings. He noticed the way she dove straight into the presentation and immediately captured the audience's attention. The stories registered. Mack was reading the audience.

Bullet Point 1: Be aware of your surroundings and the people around you.

ACTION

- The next time you sit in an audience, notice how the audience responds to the presenter. Are people checking their phones and tablets? Napping? Whispering to one another? Leaning forward? Focusing on the presenter? What do you think the presenter is doing to elicit the reaction he or she is receiving? What happens when the presenter tells a story?

A great place to start building confidence is by becoming comfortable around people. If you're presenting to a group, spend time chatting with the emcee or person introducing you prior to your time on stage. Intentionally interact with people in the audience before the event. These conversations will take your mind off the presentation, relieving anxiety and helping you better know your audience.

2

CHLOE CONNECTS

"A wise man will hear and increase learning, and a man of understanding will attain wise counsel."
—*Proverbs 1:5 NKJV*

The last speaker wrapped up his comments. The moderator walked up to the podium, thanked the presenters and the audience, and dismissed them. Polite applause lasted for a few seconds as people in the audience started rising from their seats. The sound of a thousand voices quickly filled the space.

"Maybe they'll forget I was even on the stage," Mack said to himself. Thoughts of self-doubt were paused when Mack felt a gentle touch to his elbow. He turned to see Chloe.

"I had no idea InCirq was such an important part of my phone," she said. "I really enjoyed learning about the products you're making and competition you face in such a tight market."

"Uh, you know, it's really…," Mack stammered while thinking to himself how his horrible presentation paled in comparison to Chloe's. "It's just what we do."

"Do you have a business card?" Chloe asked while offering hers. "At some point as we grow, I'd like to talk about some partnership opportunities in the manufacturing side of what we do." Mack found his card on the inside of his jacket pocket, pulled it out, and gave it to Chloe.

"Yeah, just call my office. I'd be happy to talk to you."

Mack wanted desperately to get off the stage and escape the room and everyone in it. After a few more forced smiles, handshakes, and an empty "good to see you, too," Mack looked for an exit. However, Norman Reynolds stood between him and the door. "Just when things couldn't get worse," Mack thought to himself. He walked down the stairs and up to Norman. "Hello, Mr. Reynolds. I didn't expect to see you here."

"I wouldn't miss it," Norman said. "You know, Mack, as an InCirq board member, it's my duty to let you know you do a tremendous disservice to the company when you perform like that in front of a group like this."

Mack was accustomed to Norman's quips and jabs, but he'd never been confronted by the seventy-two-year-old in such a straightforward way. "Well, um," Mack started stammering. He could only stutter "I'm sorry, Mr. Reynolds. I really need to get back to the office." He stepped to the side and started walking toward the exit.

"Have a good day," Norman stated, his words dripping with a tone of satisfaction.

His calendar was packed the rest of the day, but Mack's mind kept replaying his pitiful performance. "I should never have accepted the invite to speak," he thought. "I just confirmed to everyone that I'm not the leader people think I should be. Do I really have what it takes?"

These thoughts kept bombarding him throughout the day.

Later that night, Mack made his way down the stairs in the house he and his wife had made a home for the past twelve years. His eight-year-old son, Devon, and twelve-year-old daughter, Mikala, had already fallen fast asleep. Mack's wife, Ellie, was preparing for the nightly ritual that had become the backbone of the marriage: the evening postmortem. At this thought, Mack's lips turned up in a slight smile as he immediately started to relax. The ritual began as simply time on the couch, hashing over the day's events. When a glass of wine was added, it turned into a strong connecting point. Ellie would start with details about the kids, school, extracurricular activities, discipline issues, and new discoveries.

Mack thought of Ellie as his heart. He was the no-holds-barred business guy. "Don't give me reasons; give me results," was his mantra. She remembered names, noticed the fine details, and had amazing insight into people. She was his best friend; she completed him.

During evening postmortem, they discussed Devon's first practice with his lacrosse team and his excitement about meeting a new friend. Although Mikala was struggling with math, Ellie related that Mikala's teacher agreed to tutor her for fifteen minutes after each class to improve her skills. Ellie shared an interesting conversation she had with a friend over lunch.

Then, it was his turn. Knowing it had been a major stress point for Mack during the past several days, Ellie asked, "How did your speech go?"

"I bombed," he sighed. "If it could go wrong, it did go wrong. The PowerPoint didn't work, I froze up, and I couldn't get a complete sentence out of my mouth, I really don't want to talk about it."

"Was there anything good about the day?" Ellie asked.

"You know," Mack continued, almost ignoring the question, "after I finished, this young CEO of a start-up got on stage, and she immediately had the audience wrapped around her finger. She had people laughing and learning. I thought, 'This can't be that hard. Why do I have such a tough time getting in front of people?'"

Ellie was quiet. A moment passed.

Mack continued, "This person with a fraction of my experience can get up in front of a thousand people and just talk."

Ellie listened as Mack continued relating the day's events. "So, what do you think?"

Ellie's intuition kicked in, and she probed "How important is it for you to be able to get up in front of a group and talk?"

"It's very important."

"So, what do you need to do to improve?"

"If I could just spend some time studying a person like Chloe and asking her how she has the confidence to speak, I could learn a lot."

"So why don't you ask her?"

"It just feels awkward."

"More awkward than sweating bullets in front of a thousand people?" Ellie knew how to get straight to the heart of the matter.

"Put yourself in my position," Mack said. "I've got at least twenty years on her; I'm the COO of a multinational corporation. Isn't there the expectation that I should already know how to get up in front of a group?"

Ellie glanced up at the ceiling, looking for the right words. "Whose expectation?" She didn't pause long enough for him to answer.

"Mack, you push yourself hard. That's why you're successful. But I don't think it's fair to think everyone expects you to be an expert up on the stage."

"Yeah, but," Mack stuttered searching for words, "with my experience and age, it's embarrassing that I can't stand up there and talk to people."

Ellie said, "Mack, one of the things I love about you is your integrity. You're consistent. If you had an employee facing a challenge like this, what would you ask them to do?"

"I'd encourage them to get help."

"It seems like you have a chance to get some help."

"Okay, I'll shoot her an e-mail tomorrow."

"No," Ellie said as she reached across Mack to grab his iPad. Dropping it in his lap, she said, "How about now?"

A grin spread across Mack's face. "You know me so well," he said as he reached over to kiss Ellie.

Not five minutes after Mack hit the send button on the e-mail, Chloe responded. She would work through his assistant to schedule a time in the next two weeks for a lunch appointment.

BULLET POINTS

In his book, *The Millionaire Mind*, Thomas Stanley wrote about a research project created to identify the attributes that successful people have in common. A supportive spouse was in the top five attributes. Don't take your significant other for granted as you work to improve your presentation skills. Mack relied on Ellie. On whom can you rely? Communication requires at least two people. Improving communication is very difficult to accomplish without an accomplice.

Bullet Point 2: A strong relationship at home is an important piece in the puzzle that makes up a strong, confident presenter.

Brian Tracy, in The Power of Self-Confidence, shared the story of an engineering firm manager who approached Tracy after a speech. The manager explained he was a top performer at his firm but kept getting passed over for promotions. Tracy asked the man what his coworkers did differently. The manager explained his counterparts were strong at presenting, which translated into additional sales for the company. They were rainmakers. The engineer explained his fear of presenting to groups, arguing it shouldn't matter because of his engineering skills. Tracy convinced him otherwise and encouraged the manager to take seminars and read books on improving his presentation skills. A year later, Tracy ran into the manager and discovered he had followed the advice, joined Toastmasters, taken a Dale Carnegie course, and read several books. He had been promoted twice and increased his income by 40 percent.

Tracy wrote, "Your weakest important skill determines the height of your success in your work." Look at the research about the top skills required in the workplace, and you will find communication near or at the top. Working on your communication skills will always pay off.

Bullet Point 3: Don't be scared to ask for help. Thinking that you know it all or being too fearful to seek a coach or mentor is a dangerous frame of mind.

When you consider the high percentage of the population that becomes anxious at the thought of giving a presentation, what's the downside of asking for help? Have you ever sat in a crowd of people wanting to ask a clarifying question of the presenter? If you asked the question, more than likely, most others in the audience had the same question. If someone else asked the question, you were relieved to know you weren't the only one.

The same is true about asking for help in improving your communication skills. Most people don't like to give presentations. All listeners appreciate a skilled presenter.

ACTION

- Ask for help. Find a coach or a mentor, even if it's as simple as asking your spouse to help you improve in specific areas such as counting ums, noting distracting gestures, or reminding you to make eye contact.

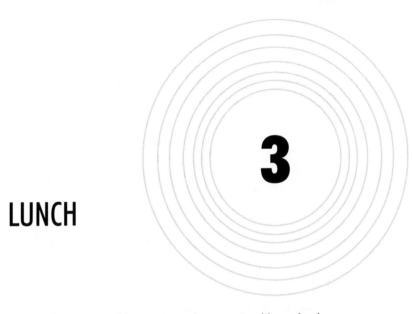

3

LUNCH

*"Character is like a tree and reputation like a shadow.
The shadow is what we think of it; the tree is the real thing."*
—Abraham Lincoln

"Mack's Meltdown" continued to replay over and over in Mack's mind. Nearly two weeks had passed since the economic forum. Being relatively new in the position, he'd never had to give a speech to a thousand people. He'd made plenty of mistakes along the way as he learned the technology business, but he viewed each step as a professional learning experience. Life's experiences had helped him advance his career from Product Engineer at InCirq to Chief Operating Officer. His journey was the epitome of the work-from-the-ground-up story. He'd accomplished so much. Why was talking to people such a stumbling block?

Mack was dreading the lunch meeting with Chloe that was just moments away. He walked through the large wood doors of the upscale restaurant where his assistant had made lunch reservations.

The lady at the front escorted Mack to a table in the center of the large, open dining area where Chloe was waiting. She stood up to greet Mack. After settling into their seats, Chloe began, "When I told you I wanted to talk about partnership ideas, I had no idea you would want to meet so soon. Thank you so much for reaching out."

"You did such a great job with your presentation at the economic forum," Mack said. "You really opened my eyes to what's going on. I think we are blinded to the local scene because we operate internationally and most of our competition on the chip side is in Asia."

Small talk about markets, professional experience, and professional acquaintances filled the brief time until the waiter arrived to take the order.

The moment the menu was taken from his hand, Mack shifted uncomfortably in his chair, and dove in. "This feels really awkward, but my wife said I needed to meet with you and ask for some help with my presentation skills." The words hung in the air even more awkwardly.

Chloe stammered briefly but quickly regained her composure. "I'm very flattered. The real question is, do you want help with your presentation skills?"

"I don't know. Well, let me put it this way. I know I need help. I'm not sure I can be helped. The thought of getting up in front of a group of people, whether my board or the economic forum a few weeks ago, scares the heck out of me."

"Why?"

"Always has. I figured it was just one of those things that was built into my DNA."

"I used to think that too." Chloe leaned in and lowered her voice slightly. "Then, I figured out a secret. It's not about me."

Mack was confused. "What do you mean, it's not about me?"

"How would you describe your leadership style at InCirq?" Chloe asked.

Mack had spent time training on coaching style and immediately recognized Chloe's tactic. She was asking questions, leading him to find the answers on his own. He admired that and knew it was in his best interest to answer to the best of his ability. "I haven't thought about that in a long time," he said. "If I had to choose words to describe it, I'd say collaborative, open, and innovative. I see myself as the person who removes the obstacles so the people on my team can do their job."

Chloe fired off the next question. "Do you see yourself as a servant leader?"

Mack said, "Yeah, I guess that description works based on what I just told you."

"There's a question I love to ask myself as I'm getting ready to give a presentation. Am I more in love with the topic than the people?" Chloe sat silently for a moment letting Mack contemplate the question.

Chloe continued with a story. "This idea really hit when I was working on the road and needed to get my hair done. I found a salon with great reviews and was able to get a same-day appointment with the owner. As we were talking, she asked if I was familiar with the salon philosophy. I wasn't. She said, 'We want you to walk out a better version of you.'"

Chloe noticed Mack looked a little confused. She continued, "She didn't want to remake me or turn me into a new person. She wanted to make me a better version of me. As a presenter who really cares about my audience, I want people to leave as a better version of themselves. That keeps my priorities in the right place."

Chloe saw understanding dawn in Mack's reaction. He got it. It was time to lighten up a bit. After this profound thought, Chloe went back to small talk, asking about family and recreation. As the food arrived, the two continued chatting.

Mack finished the meal first. As the waiter took the empty plate, Mack said, "I'd like to hire you to coach me on presentation skills."

The blunt request took Chloe off guard since she didn't see herself as a presentation coach. "What exactly do you have in mind?" she asked.

"I have some major presentations coming up in the next several months," Mack explained. "I'd like to meet once a week for at least two months to get ready. I know it's a big time commitment, but I don't know where to turn. I'll pay whatever you think is fair."

"I'm not thinking about the money," Chloe responded quickly, "but if we're going to invest that kind of time, I want to be sure I can actually help you."

"You already have. You're a natural coach."

"I'm honored and will have to accept. It should be fun."

"Deal." Mack pulled out his phone. "My assistant hates it when I put things in my calendar, but let's set an appointment. Would you be willing to meet in our conference room?"

"Works for me." Chloe was also looking through the calendar on her phone. "How about next Thursday at ten in the morning?"

"Can't do that. How about two that afternoon?"

"No, but I could be there by four."

LUNCH

"This is why Mary, my assistant, doesn't want me messing with my calendar. Are you open to video conferencing?"

"Absolutely. I do a lot of meetings via video."

"Great. As soon as I get back to the office, I'll have Mary contact you to figure out a time in the next week. I have a feeling she knows which of these appointments can be postponed or moved around to open up time for us."

"Sounds like a great idea."

The waiter slipped in to take Chloe's plate and asked if the two would be having dessert. Both said no and Mack asked for the bill.

"Thank you for considering this," Mack said.

Chloe responded, "No, thank you for asking. This will be a great experience." She looked at her watch, "Oh, I'm supposed to be on a conference call. Thank you so much for lunch. We'll talk soon." She stood up and reached out to shake Mack's hand.

"Thank you," Mack said. "Oh, and by the way, keep those partnership ideas on the front burner. I'm definitely interested."

BULLET POINTS

If you think there's no hope or help to get you past your fear of public speaking, think again. There lives in most of us the desire to see people win. We cheer for the underdog. We root for the one who struggles the most. People want to see you succeed when you give a presentation. Feed off that knowledge. Use that knowledge to reach out to those who demonstrate competent presentation skills. Ask the accomplished presenters you know for help. Go to lunch. Arrange a coffee.

> **Bullet Point 4: Remind yourself that most people want to see you present well.**

If you've fallen for the politically correct nonsense that your private life does not affect your public life, and you can be the equivalent of different people depending on your surroundings, think again. While moral relativism might be a nice cop-out for some, it doesn't work in the real world of ethical leadership.

Integrity is a must. In the Bullet Points of chapter 2, I referred to *The Millionaire Mind*, by Thomas Stanley. His research project revealed the top five characteristics of the most successful people. Integrity is the number one trait. My personal definition for integrity is simple: Think = Say = Do. What is done out of sight (thinking) is consistent with what I say and is consistent with what I do. It all matches. To be a relevant, trusted, believable presenter, you must have integrity, which is in alignment with your public and private life.

Truly effective communicators have integrity. What's thought is the same as what's said, which is the same as what's done. Consistent character counts.

ACTION

- What is your personal definition of integrity? Write it. Live it.

Bullet Point 5: Embrace the paradigm shift. Your presentation isn't about you; it's about the audience. Are you more in love with the topic than the people? If so, change your priorities.

As you consider the implication of Bullet Point 5, I need to stress that the most engaging presenters are passionate about the topic on which they are speaking. A part of the palpable passion is the desire to share and enrich the audience. A presenter who is in love with the topic really doesn't care if he or she imparts knowledge to the audience. Be passionate about the subject, but not myopically in love; always put the people first.

ACTION

- As you prepare for your next presentation , whether it's an audience of one, ten, one hundred, or one thousand, complete the statement, "I want people in the audience to walk away from the presentation with . . ." Limit yourself to one thing (don't create a bullet list) that genuinely makes each person in the audience a better version.

LAW OF PRESENTING: #1

Character Counts.

What you do in private matters. It will be revealed in public someday, somehow, somewhere.

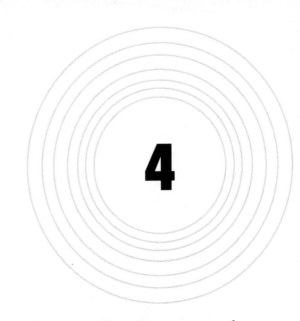

LESSONS

4

"You are the same today as you will be in five years except for the people you meet and the books you read."
—Charlie "Tremendous" Jones

As he drove from the restaurant, Mack was on the phone with his wife, sharing details of his lunchtime conversation with Chloe. Ellie let him know she was thrilled about the coaching sessions.

When Mack walked into his office, he explained the plan of attack to improve his presentation skills with his assistant, Mary. He asked Mary to set up the first meeting with Chloe. "Ask her if we can use video conferencing please."

Later in the day, Mary poked her head in the door to say all was a go with Chloe. She was sending an e-mail with a homework assignment, and a Skype call was scheduled for the next week.

As promised, the e-mail arrived later that night. The subject read, "The good, bad, and ugly of presenting." Immediately, Mack's curiosity was piqued.

"Let's start by looking at different presentation styles," Chloe's e-mail began. "Watch how people present themselves. What captures your attention? What annoys you? Pay attention at work, set time aside to watch presentations online, and pay attention to how the pastor engages the audience if you go to church.

"There are a few specific things I want you to see in preparation for next week's conversation.

"First, do an Internet search for Simon Sinek: How great leaders inspire action. You'll find an eighteen-minute video from September 2009. Don't let the age of the video fool you. The content is rich with things for you to consider as you start putting the audience first and understanding how people think and what drives them to act. You'll also notice his strong presentation skills.

"Read. Read fiction. Read nonfiction. Read blogs. Read for enjoyment and read to learn. Reading spreadsheets and InCirq reports don't count. The more you read, the better you'll master the English language. Andy Andrews is a masterful storyteller and speaker. Reading his work and watching him on YouTube will give you some great ideas to craft stories of your own. If you don't already, I'd recommend you subscribe to and read Seth Godin's daily blog and Josh Linkner's weekly blog. Also, follow them on Twitter: @sethgodin and @joshlinkner.

"I'm also a big believer in starting with the end in mind. So, let's work toward a goal. You mentioned you have some presentations coming up. Let me know what it is you're preparing for so we can work toward getting you ready."

The week passed quickly. Mack and Chloe met via Skype.

"How's it going?" Chloe asked.

"Okay, I guess," Mack hesitated. "I'll tell you now, there's no way I'll be like any of those people you told me to watch."

"Ah, lesson number one," Chloe said with a smile. "The only reason you watch, read, and listen is to study technique. The moment you try to be somebody else, you fail. You must be your genuine, authentic, real self. Mack, you've got to be you."

Mack interrupted, "Being me is what caused me so much trouble at the economic forum. I feel like I'm my own worst enemy. I can't imagine anything about me that makes me a good presenter." The booming voice of self-doubt that echoed through Mack's thoughts came pouring out of his mouth. "I really think this might all be a waste of time."

"Wait a minute," Chloe interjected, stopping him in his tracks. "What are you good at?"

There was silence as Mack stared at the image of his face on his computer screen. He contemplated Chloe's question, repeating it silently in his mind.

"Mack," Chloe said, "this is a confidence issue. As an outsider who doesn't know you, I can list off some of the things you're good at. That won't do you any good. You need to say the things you know beyond a shadow of doubt to be true about you."

"Okay," Mack replied exasperated. "I know I'm good at my job. I know I'm one of the top chief operating officers in the country, if not the world." Mack paused. "That's really uncomfortable."

"I know," Chloe said. "Your humility is one of the attributes that makes you a strong leader. Saying it out loud doesn't make you less humble. Just work with me here."

"It's still uncomfortable," Mack said. "I'm also a faithful husband, and I do my best to be a good dad. I'm a strong leader. My team respects me."

"Were you born with all those attributes?" Chloe asked.

"No, of course not," Mack said.

Chloe began her reasoning. "Those traits took time. No talent, skill, or knowledge happens automatically. It takes time to become good at something, whether it's being a dad or a COO." She paused and looked at Mack. She could still read the lack of confidence in his face. "Do you know if you know the right stuff?"

The abrupt question confused Mack. "Uh, I'm sorry. Would you repeat that?"

"Do you know if you know the right stuff?" Chloe asked. "Do you know if you have what it takes to be COO?"

"Well, I never thought about it like that, but yes," Mack responded slowly, working through each word, hoping he did not sound arrogant. "There's a reason I'm where I'm at in my life and in my career. I guess I know I know the right stuff."

"Then, if you're confident you know the right stuff," Chloe said, feeling like she was making progress, "you need to feel that same type of confidence when you're presenting."

"That's my problem," Mack interjected. "I've spent years learning, practicing, and studying to get where I'm at as COO. I'm not there with my presentation skills."

"You're wrong." Chloe shot back, watching Mack's image on her computer screen intently for his reaction. Mack wasn't used to being told he was wrong. He sat in stunned silence. Chloe could tell she had to strike quickly to make her point. "Mack, you've been practicing presenting more than you've practiced anything else in your life. Every conversation you have, every time you speak, every time you listen, you're practicing your presentation skills. Presenting is nothing more than having a conversation. The only difference is the number of people listening and the format of the presentation." She paused, watching the contemplative look on Mack's face.

Chloe tapped keys on her keyboard and shared her computer screen with Mack. "Take a look at this," she said. She opened her web browser and typed two words in the Google search engine: definition communication.

com·mu·ni·ca·tion
/kə͵myōōniˈkāSHən/ ◄))

Noun
1. The imparting or exchanging of information or news.
2. A letter or message containing such information or news.

Synonyms
connection - message - connexion - intercourse

Google returned 194,000,000 results in 0.15 seconds. "Read number one," Chloe said.

Mack read aloud, "The imparting or exchanging of information or news."

Chloe followed up quickly. "Now, replace the word 'imparting' with 'sharing' and read it again."

Mack did as instructed, "The sharing or exchanging of information or news."

"There you have it," Chloe said. "Isn't presenting just sharing information or news? Isn't a conversation with your wife just sharing information or news? Isn't talking with your assistant just sharing information? And, isn't what you did in front of the crowd at the economic forum a couple weeks ago also just sharing information?"

"Okay, yeah, I get it," Mack conceded. "But, it doesn't make it any easier."

Chloe leaned in toward the camera and lowered her voice. "Mack, the problem isn't with your lack of knowledge or practice; it's in the massive roadblock you've created in your mind about presenting."

Mack brought both hands to his face, rubbing his cheeks in a way that made him look like he'd had enough.

"Everyone finds their confidence as a presenter in a different way and at a different time," Chloe said. "We're going to find ways to tap into the confidence you have in other areas of your life to help you build the confidence to be a great presenter."

Chloe looked at the clock in the corner of her computer screen. "We need to wrap this up. I want to circle back to where we started by looking at other presenters and reading."

The conversation had sapped Mack's energy. He'd experienced much more intense, longer-lasting exchanges in negotiating billion-dollar deals, mergers, and acquisitions. "Those 'communication' sessions," he thought to himself, "weren't nearly as difficult as the work of self-introspection." He was ready for an end to the session.

"Remember," Chloe said, "watching other presenters is not about copying technique. What did you notice about Simon Sinek?"

Thinking back to the video, Mack searched for something meaningful to say. "He was passionate about the topic, and he told a lot of stories."

"Did you notice his use of repetition?" Chloe asked.

"Yes," Mack said. "People don't buy what you do; they buy why you do it."

"You remember," Chloe said with a grin. "Did the repetition drive you crazy?"

Mack thought about it. "No, it didn't bother me. He was so conversational that I didn't notice him constantly saying, 'People don't buy what you do; they buy why you do it.'"

Chloe repeated Mack's observation, "Conversational?"

Mack looked at Chloe's image on his computer screen, trying to figure out how the word "conversational" could be a question.

Chloe saw the confusion and quickly clarified. "Aren't you conversational when you talk to your wife, your assistant, or colleagues?"

"Yes," Mack said, instantly understanding the point.

"Okay," Chloe signaled an end to the conversation, "you also mentioned stories. For our next conversation, I want you to think of a story you can use to illustrate a point for that presentation we are working toward. By the way, when is your next presentation? Whom are you talking to?"

"I think it's about a month away," Mack answered. "We're rolling out a new video blog, and I'll be doing a live video cast to all the InCirq employees."

"Great," Chloe said. "In the next week, I'd like you to come up with at least two stories you can share. They need to be personal and true."

"But how do I find them?" Mack asked.

"You'll figure it out," Chloe responded with a smile. "I've got to go."

BULLET POINTS

Why do we get so caught up in the fear of speaking in public? Unfortunately, it's part of the human condition. Your confidence as a presenter starts when you get to know yourself really well. What are you good at? Do you know if you know the right stuff? Know the answer to those questions, and you'll have the starting point of being a better version of you on the stage, in the boardroom, or in a client's office giving a presentation.

There's a reason you were chosen to present. You have talent, skills, and knowledge. You're confident in your role at home, in the office, or in the community. Do you have confidence when speaking with your spouse, a friend, colleague, coworker, or employee? I'm venturing a guess that the answer is yes. Why should communicating your talent, skills, and knowledge to a different audience be any different? Communication is the act of sharing information. The information doesn't change based on who's receiving the information you're sharing. Although the stakes and the number of people receiving your message might be higher, rely on the confidence you have in the subject matter at hand.

Bullet Point 6: Reading builds your vocabulary and communication skills. Be a voracious reader.

ACTION

- What is your personal definition of integrity? Write it. Live it.

Bullet Point 7: Connect the confidence you have in your knowledge and the confidence you have in communicating on an interpersonal level with family, friends, and coworkers.

ACTION

- Invest the time to shift the paradigm in your mind: sharing information is sharing information, regardless of the audience size. When communicating, you should take your communication with a loved one, friend, or acquaintance as seriously as you do with a presentation.

LAW OF PRESENTING: #2

Be real, authentic, and genuine.

It's redundant for a reason. Being yourself is critical to your success. People have a tuned-in "fake" meter. Set that meter off, and you lose the audience.

LAW OF PRESENTING: #3

Seek Wisdom.

Continually growing your knowledge and putting it into practice will build skills and grow talents.

SWEATING BULLETS

While we're talking about seeking wisdom, continual learning, and gaining confidence in knowing the right stuff, please stay humble. Plato said, "The learning and knowledge that we have is, at the most, but little compared with that of which we are ignorant."

5

FINDING STORIES

"My stories run up and bite me on the leg—I respond by writing down everything that goes on during the bite. When I finish, the idea lets go and runs off."
—Ray Bradbury

The clock read 11:45 p.m. Leaning against the headboard of his bed, Mack was wide awake, while Ellie slept soundly beside him. The white glow of the iPad illuminated the area around him.

Mack used a smart pen to take notes and write ideas. Every stroke of the pen on the special notebook paper was captured and uploaded to his Evernote account. He was searching through notes, looking for any scribble that would jar his memory and reveal a story he could use for his presentation to the InCirq employees.

Only two weeks of preparation time remained.

Mack swiped at the screen, looking at notes from the meetings he had attended. He was searching for stories that would illustrate the importance of the video blog. As he read through his notes, he noticed a phrase. There, on the digitized page, circled and underlined, were two words: Modern Mentoring. The memory came flooding back. Mack had attended a human resources conference years ago. One of the many presenters had captured the audience, leading people to a greater understanding of engaging and mentoring employees. During a portion of the talk, the presenter put an image on the screen and talked about ways leaders can become more aware of the needs around them or discover the "evident." "So often," the speaker claimed, "people don't see the obvious, for any number of reasons."

Mack had used his phone to snap a photo of the screen during the presentation.

The presenter explained that NASA had provided the photo. It was satellite picture of someplace on the globe. The presenter asked the audience, "Where is it?" People in the audience threw out guesses of South America and Africa. Then, the speaker said, "I often hear guesses like that. But let me point out the eyes of the cow, and here's the nose." People gasped as the evident was revealed before their eyes.

"Where are the opportunities in your organization?" the speaker asked. "So often, the answer you need to solve the pressing problem is right in front of you. You may need to change your perspective, ask for help, or open your mind to possibilities 'outside the box,' but this little exercise proves how often the real answer is right under your nose."

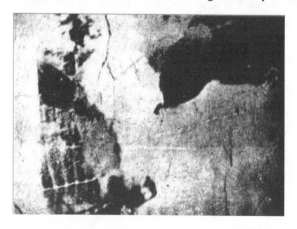

FINDING STORIES

Mack felt the exciting sense of realizing the obvious. The stories were all around him. He needed to change his mind-set to be able to discover the evident. As he skimmed the notes from the meeting, Mack thought back to a recent car purchase. He and Ellie didn't like to drive the expensive European luxury machines his counterparts often chose, but he and Ellie did want something a little different than the most common cars on the road. They shopped and decided on what they thought was a slightly unique car. On the drive home, they discovered the obvious. The car wasn't unique. In a five-mile stretch of busy road, the two counted six cars that were the same model as the one they just bought. Two of the six were the same year and color. "I guess we're not that unique after all," he remembered telling his wife.

After that, the running joke was for the kids to sit in the back seat on drives, pointing out to mom and dad the number of cars on the road of the same make and model. The kids earned extra points in the game if they spotted the same color, make, model, and year. Mack smiled, thinking about the simplicity of the concept. Stories were all around him; he just needed to pay attention.

Mack's index finger instinctively found its way to the top right edge of the iPad, where he pressed the button to black out the screen. He sat in the quiet darkness of the bedroom thinking.

"That's it," he thought to himself, remembering a story that would definitely illustrate the importance of the video blog for InCirq's team.

Mack was a big fan of Jason Jennings, a business consultant, speaker, and author. Jennings had written about ways to create a culture of growth in any organization through the story of Yellow Freight. Newly minted CEO Bill Zollars had taken over a company he knew would be bankrupt within eighteen months if drastic changes weren't made. Employee morale was dismal. The company culture had been reduced to an us-versus-them mentality. Zollar decided to turn the stodgy, old school freight company into a logistics company. To initiate the change, Zollar started visiting freight terminals all over the country. Within a year and a half, he had met with thousands of the twenty-five thousand employees, explaining the changes that needed to be made and setting the stage for growth in a new business model.

Mack had taken this story to heart, traveling to InCirq's offices around the globe and meeting with as many people as possible. While InCirq was nowhere near the critical juncture that Yellow Freight was, it was in a highly competitive, commoditized industry. "It takes the right people, in the right positions, doing the right things to make InCirq stay competitive, grow, and provide a winning experience for all employees," Mack had told his management team. The trips and meetings were exhausting but set InCirq on the course to success.

Mack saw the video blogs as the next iteration of the face-to-face meetings. He also knew a message couldn't be delivered just once. It had to be repeated over and over again.

During the initial tour of face-to-face meetings, Mack was sitting in the break room of InCirq's offices in Ulsoor, India. About twenty-five people had gathered to hear Mack explain why the company exists and what its core values are.

At the close of Mack's conversation with the group, Abiah, an employee in her midtwenties, timidly approached him. "This was so helpful," Abiah said. "I have been offered a job that pays a little more with a competitor in another city here in India. I was seriously considering it because I thought I was just another cog in the wheel and no one really cared about what I have to offer, but I've changed my mind. After hearing what you said, I want to be a part of InCirq."

That conversation had played over in Mack's mind numerous times. He knew he must improve his presentation and communication skills so that he would be able to connect with, explain himself to, and win the hearts and minds of the fifteen thousand members of the worldwide InCirq team. It was Abiah's words in a break room in Ulsoor that led to the video blog. Mack wanted to provide a constant reminder of why each person was so important to the success of InCirq. He decided this story was the one he would tell in the inaugural video blog.

BULLET POINTS

Why have we abandoned the gift of learning through storytelling? As children, we learned so many lessons through stories. This is the reason you're not reading just another prescriptive book on the twelve steps to give an effective presentation. Wouldn't you rather read a story?

As I speak to audiences, I often pose the question, "You have a choice right now. You can go to a meeting at your office or go to a movie. Which is it?" Invariably, 99.9 percent of the audience will choose the movie.

I immediately respond, "So, let me get this straight. You have a choice between gathering with a group of people you know in a clean, well-lit, and comfortable place to talk, share, and work on something meaningful. But you're choosing to go sit in a dark room with strangers, feeling your feet stick to the floor that's covered in soda and popcorn?" Doesn't the story make all the difference?

You can hear facts, figures, and statistics and read spreadsheets ad nauseam. Does any of it stick with you? No. If you hear a story, your mind instantly engages. You're imagining the setting and the people. Stories enable people to remember history. Encouraging re-gurgitation rather than promoting critical thinking, History teachers who just require and test on memorization of facts and dates do a disservice to students. But when students learn the story behind the history, they remember it forever. Storytelling is the one constant throughout all of human history.

Bullet Point 8: As human beings, our minds are wired to learn from and respond to stories. If you want the information you present to be memorable, tell a story.

ACTION

- Inventory your stories. Get in the habit of discovering the evident. The stories are all around you. Keep a handwritten journal. Use Evernote, a free web-based, note-taking, and archiving application. It is easy to use and makes your notes available on your computer, tablet, or smartphone. Put a file folder for loose notepaper in a drawer. Use whatever system works best for you to capture and catalog stories so that you don't forget the most important learning tools in your arsenal.

At the heart of every good story are three simple pieces: challenge, struggle, and resolution. Look how simple it played out with Abiah. Her challenge was feeling unappreciated, which led to the struggle of deciding whether to move to another city in India to find a more rewarding job. She found resolution in hearing Mack's compelling message. Challenge, struggle, and resolution are what your story needs.

ACTION

- When planning your next presentation, include at least one story for every point you want people to remember.

LAW OF PRESENTING: #4

Tell stories.

Stories are memorable and will make the information you share in a presentation memorable. Illustrate every point you want to make with a story.

AUDIENCE FIRST

"The whole point of telling a purposeful story is to energize audiences around your mission or cause, and if your presentation sucks the energy out of them, then you've defeated your purpose."
—Peter Guber, *Tell to Win: Connect, Persuade, and Triumph with the Hidden Power of Story*

Mack's assistant, Mary, peeked her head in through his door. "Chloe is waiting for you in the conference room," she said.

Mack had been caught up in a number of conference calls and had forgotten about the meeting. Fortunately, he'd been so excited by the epiphany of figuring out stories that he was ready for today's conversation.

Chloe stood up and shot out her hand as Mack walked in the room. After a quick handshake, both sat down.

"Well," Chloe got straight to the point, "tell me the two stories you discovered."

Mack quickly relayed the story of Abiah in Ulsoor, India. Chloe asked a few clarifying questions and encouraged Mack to share his second story. Mack jumped right in. "After discovering the importance of connecting with people on a more relational level during my trips to our offices all over the world, I was at a loss at how to continue the connection. I was literally waking up in the night, trying to figure out a way to communicate face to face with so many people in so many different places at so many different times. I knew there was no way I could maintain the travel schedule or expect anyone else to do it for me.

"The frustration continued to build as I looked for an answer. About a month after I returned from the last trip, I was in a meeting with the research and development folks. They had been tasked with developing new apps that would showcase and make the most of our chips and other hardware. The team members went around the room sharing progress reports. Mostly, it was status reports because there wasn't much progress."

Mack paused briefly and looked at Chloe. She was genuinely smiling at Mack's attempt at humor.

Mack continued. "After the meeting, one of the R & D folks, Mike, walked up and asked if I had a moment. My reply was yes. He said that while he was working on the apps and trying to find other uses for our technology, he thought he had made a mistake in testing one of our chips. But as he looked more closely, he discovered our chip worked really well configured with a highly miniaturized high-definition camera developed by one of our partners in Japan. Since the discovery was outside the realm of what the R & D group had been tasked to accomplish and involved another company's product, he didn't want to share the story in our meeting. I asked him what he was able to do with his discovery, and that's when his eyes lit up. He said he enlisted the help of his sixteen-year-old daughter, and the two wrote some code one night for a new video compression codec."

"While I might be the COO of InCirq, it doesn't take long for technical people to start talking over my head. I could tell he was getting more excited about the discovery, so I asked him to continue, but to use plain English.

"He said that all of this had happened in the past twenty-four hours. With this new high-definition codec, he thought he could write a new video capture and sharing app. He wanted to give it a try but wasn't sure it was in the scope of his job description.

"We're really working to foster an open, collaborative, and innovative culture at InCirq. Mike's willingness to share his idea with me shows that we really are who we're working to be.

"I told him he had done a great job of connecting the dots to figure out new uses for our technology, because it was probably our chip connected to our partner's camera that would make his idea work. I shared the story with his manager and gave both the encouragement to forge ahead.

"About a week later, I received a strange pop-up on my iPhone. Our IT folks had been brought in on the new project and had loaded an app on my phone, unbeknownst to me. When I saw the alert on my phone, I swiped the screen and up popped this video of Mike, telling me the new technology was ready for beta testing. When I looked at the screen, I figured out it was the app that Mike had built. It was so intuitive. I pushed a button, recorded a message back to Mike, congratulating him on the success of his app, hit send, and then saw other videos he had loaded in a library on the app.

"I tell the story to illustrate the power of innovation and collaboration in InCirq. We're in this together. At first, Mike thought he had a flop on his hands. He had actually solved a big problem for me and most likely created a significant revenue stream for the company. And that's the story behind how you'll be hearing from me on a more regular basis through a video blog."

"Wow!" Chloe exclaimed. "You did it. I asked you to find two stories to share and...," she paused for just a moment. "You did it. Nice work."

"Thank you," Mack said.

Chloe asked why he chose these two stories. "They illustrate the points I'm trying to make," Mack responded.

"Is there anything else?" Chloe asked.

"I really didn't give it much thought," Mack said. "I was just happy to stumble on a couple of stories that would work for the presentation."

"What do you think those stories will mean to your audience?" Chloe asked, moving into coaching mode.

Mack was a bit perplexed. What was Chloe getting at? "I guess, I hope they like the stories." Mack said, making the statement sound more like a question.

"It sounds like you stumbled on one of the cardinal rules of giving a presentation," Chloe said, smiling. "Audience first." She paused to let the two words sink in. "Audience first is the rule that can never be broken. It's about creating a connection with the people with whom you're speaking."

Mack was processing the two words: *audience first*. Chloe persisted, "Think of each person in the audience as having an emotional fuel tank. As the presenter, you can drain the tank or fill the tank. Which would you rather do?"

"I'd rather fill the tank," Mack said.

Chloe smiled. "Exactly. So, if before you even start the presentation, whether it's to one, ten, one hundred, or one thousand people, what if you start thinking about each person's emotional fuel tank? How does that change your perspective?"

Mack thought for a few moments. "It would definitely take my mind off of me and how nervous I am."

"That's true. But, it's not just another tool to get your mind off of being nervous. If that's all we wanted to do, I'd give you the horrible advice to imagine every person in the room sitting there in their underwear."

Mack was starting to observe Chloe's timing, use of humor, and ways she punctuated important points with pauses and changes in volume and tone. He thought to himself that there was plenty to learn by just paying attention to beyond what she was saying.

"While it's good to get your mind off yourself," Chloe continued, "what we're really talking about is getting your mind focused on making the audience your first priority. Giving a presentation is not about you. It's about filling the emotional fuel tank of each person with whom you're communicating."

"How do I do that?"

"I have a question I like to keep in the forefront of my mind: Am I more in love with the content or the people? If you get so caught up in the content, you'll forget about the people and they'll quickly figure it out and disengage. They won't pay attention to the content—no matter how good it is."

"Are you sure?" Mack squinted his eyes to show he was not convinced.

"The Golden Rule works in every situation. You are proof that what I'm saying is true. I'll bet in the moments leading up to our meeting today that you were caught up in some other task and had forgotten about this appointment."

Mack looked a bit sheepish. "Um," he stammered a moment. "I was caught slightly off guard when Mary stuck her head in my door to say you were here. How did you know that?"

"Because I know human nature. I know you're busy. I know you have multiple demands on your time. I know you have not been sitting at your desk for the past hour studying, rehearsing, and planning for this conversation. That's not the way people behave. Your mind is finely tuned in to radio station WIIFM." She paused.

"There she goes again," Mack thought to himself. "She's good. She talks for a few moments, says something a bit provocative to capture my attention, and then stops. I'm hooked. She even leaned in a bit and lowered the volume of her voice like she was sharing a big secret about this WIIFM radio station."

"What's that?" Mack asked aloud.

"What's In It For Me." Chloe said. "Your frame of reference, my frame of reference, everyone's frame of reference really begins with, what's in it for me. That's human nature. Sure, people can say they're better than that, but think about it. You ask yourself that question a lot."

Everything in Mack wanted to argue that he was not that self-centered. He paused to think. Yes, in full, transparent honesty, he did ask himself that question often.

"But," Mack said. "You said the Golden Rule. What does the Golden Rule have to do with people being self-centered?"

"What is the Golden Rule?" Chloe asked.

"Do unto others as you would have them do unto you."

"So if you know you're tuned in to WIIFM, and you know people in your audience are tuned in to WIIFM, and you begin by putting the audience first and filling the emotional fuel tank of each person with whom you're sharing, what do you have to do?"

"I'm going to have to be a lot more empathetic," Mack said, immediately rubbing his forehead with his outstretched thumb and forefinger, nearly reaching the temples on each side of his head in a sign of exasperation.

"Excellent choice of words," Chloe said sincerely. "People want to connect. Connection requires empathy. It's important to not confuse empathy with sympathy. No one wants you to feel sorry for them."

Mack put his hands back on top of the table, signaling he was starting to accept the concept.

"I like to think of it this way," Chloe explained. "I'm busy. I have family and work obligations. I'm either going into, in the midst of, or coming out of some type of crisis. It might not be a crisis to anyone else, but no matter how insignificant it is, it's about to be, is, or soon will be a crisis. Everyone is the same. I need to realize that part of human nature is inside of each person in the audience. Their minds are probably somewhere else. It's putting yourself in their shoes because you're the same. So, applying the Golden Rule, what would you want?"

Mack stared blankly at Chloe for just a moment. Shaking his head, almost trying to shake off the uncertainty, he said, "I, uh, I don't know."

"Let's start with what you don't want. Do you want someone to be condescending and talk down to you?"

"No."

"Do you want someone to hide behind a podium or slump in a chair at the end of a conference room table and mumble?"

"No."

"Do you want someone to read from notes or, worse yet, read from a PowerPoint slide?"

"No."

"Get the idea? Every single action you make, everything about your appearance, every mannerism, every word, *everything* is an opportunity to fill or deplete a person's emotional fuel tank. That's why people come first. Your audience is first priority."

Chloe waited for the words to sink in.

"When you say it like that, you're right," Mack conceded. "The person leading a conversation or giving a presentation has a responsibility to be sure those involved in the communication are in the best mind-set possible to receive the communication. It's really Leadership 101."

"What do you mean?"

Mack was processing the epiphany he was experiencing about the effective presenter–leadership connection. "If you've read anything from John Maxwell to Stephen Covey to Matthew Kelly, you know that so many of the leadership lessons are the same. Leaders need to put people first. Servant leaders have so much more success; they get a lot more done."

Chloe caught on quickly, "Isn't it amazing how common sense is relevant in every walk of life, whether we're talking leadership or presenting?" She paused. "When you really think about it, leaders have a responsibility to be great communicators and great communicators are leaders. You can't have one without the other."

"I really have been making this way too complicated." Mack said with a new realization. "Presenting is communicating and it doesn't matter if I'm communicating with one, ten, one hundred, or one thousand. The principles remain the same. It's important for me as a leader to grasp this, and I need to figure out how to get my mind past this notion that presenting is somehow different than the communication I'm engaged with in every other aspect of my life."

Chloe smiled. "You've got it, Mack. That was a great summary."

Mack's expression was more serious. "But," he was collecting the words in his mind, "let's go back to the presentation at the economic outlook conference. What are some ways I can put the audience first in that situation?"

Chloe searched her memory for an illustrative story to share. "Well, last time we talked, you said you were a fan of Jason Jennings. I hadn't heard of him before, so I went and looked him up. One of the videos on his website is an opening to a speech he gives. In the beginning, he explains how, before giving the presentation, he interviews people whom he knows will be in the audience. Then, he builds the presentation around the responses to those interviews. That's a powerful way to put the audience first in a few ways."

Mack responded, filling in the blanks, "Yeah, I think of a line I heard once, 'People will find you interesting when they know you're interested in them.' What better way to show the audience that you're prepared to put them first than to illustrate it by customizing the message for the audience? I don't know how many canned presentations I've heard that never took the audience into account."

"Exactly! So, if we apply the emotional fuel tank principle, what happens to the needle on the gauge when people know someone is genuinely interested in them?"

"The needle moves closer to full,"

The two sat in the quiet of the conference room, Mack staring at the bright blue sky outside. Chloe noticed Mary pointing at her wrist. Chloe pushed the button on her phone to wake it up. The hour had flown by. "Wow, that hour went fast," she said. "Listen, I need to hit the road. I'll touch base with Mary to set up our next appointment. I think you made some real progress in the area of self-confidence. We'll dig a bit deeper on ways you can build your confidence around presenting the next time we meet."

"Chloe," Mack said, standing up and reaching out his hand. "This is such a huge help. I can't thank you enough for making the time to open my eyes to some obvious truths about presenting. Thank you."

Chloe reciprocated, extending her hand for the good-bye hand-shake. "I learn something new every day about communication. I'm enjoying this learning journey with you."

BULLET POINTS

It's not about you. When you get to the place where you and your message take a backseat to the people with whom you're communicating, you will have arrived at a new paradigm as a presenter.

People have an amazing inherent ability to detect the disingenuous.

Let me explain. If you enter into the communication process with ulterior motives, with a prescriptive approach gained from some twelve-step sales training on how to get people to do what you want them to do, you'll be sniffed out by those in your audience. Think about how good you are at finding fake people. Does much get past you? No. And if an inauthentic person does get something by you once, you soon figure it out and don't give them another chance. Don't be the inauthentic, disingenuous person you stick in the stereotypical category of a used car salesman. The authenticity of putting people first is the essence of Law of Presenting 5. The law must be applied out of the foundation of Law 2: Be Real, Authentic, and Genuine.

Bullet Point 9: Being a good communicator is rooted in servant leadership.

Robert K. Greenleaf, in *The Servant as Leader*, explained the principle: "A servant-leader focuses primarily on the growth and well-being of people and the communities to which they belong. The servant-leader shares power, puts the needs of others first, and helps people develop and perform as highly as possible." Study the concept and think about the ways you can incorporate the servant–leader principles in your life. Once established as habits, they'll become evident in your presentation style.

ACTION

- Before your next presentation, ask yourself, "Do I care about the people in the audience—really, sincerely care?"

Bullet Point 10: Do your homework. People know you care by your actions and the amount of time you invest in getting to know those with whom you are communicating.

Before leaving this section on Audience First, I want to share a piece from Sun Tzu's *Art of War*. I took artistic license to change a few words (italicized).

If you know the *audience* and know yourself, you need not fear the result of a hundred *presentations*.

If you know yourself but not the *audience*, for every *successful presentation, you will have a flop*.

If you know neither the *audience* nor yourself, you will *fail as a presenter*.

LAW OF PRESENTING: #5

Audience first.

Period.

7

THE ONE QUESTION

"The person who makes a success of living is the one who sees his goal steadily and aims for it unswervingly. That is dedication."
—Cecil B. DeMille

"Did you ever read Stephen R. Covey's *The 7 Habits of Highly Effective People*?" Chloe asked Mack.

Her face was illuminated by the glow of her iPad screen in the dark room. Eight o'clock Saturday evening was the only time she and Mack could schedule a Skype chat for a session before his Monday presentation to the twenty-four people who made up the InCirq leadership team.

Mack sat in his home office. He'd already let Chloe know this needed to be shorter than usual because he didn't want to be away from his family for too long.

"It's been years," Mack replied. "But, yes. Why?"

"Do you remember the second habit?"

"Hold on," Mack replied walking away from his computer. Chloe could hear his voice echoing through the room, becoming just a little more distant. "My bookcase is right next to the desk. I can see the book. Let me grab it really quick."

Mack was back in his seat moments later.

"Reread the chapter sometime in the near future," Chloe said. "There's a sentence toward the beginning of the chapter that reads, 'Start with a clear understanding of your destination.' While Covey is writing about big life lessons, the principle also applies to presenting, and I believe it's a powerful way to build confidence."

"Okay," Mack said. "Help me understand how knowing the end from the beginning is a confidence builder."

"If I were to give you the keys to a car and tell you to start driving because you'll get to the destination in one hour, with no instructions, no map, no directions, how much confidence would you have in me and the trip you were going to take? If you had passengers, how confident would they be in the trip?"

"Not very," Mack furrowed his eyebrows, trying to figure out where Chloe was going with the analogy.

"If you don't have a clear understanding of what you will deliver to the audience, how much confidence will you have in the presentation?" Chloe followed immediately with another rhetorical question. "And, if you don't have confidence in the presentation because you don't see the end from the beginning, how will the audience feel?"

"Anyone paying attention will realize I don't know what I'm talking about." Mack now saw the natural progression of Chloe's line of questioning. "They'll see right through me."

"Think of it this way," Chloe said. "Every trip needs a road map. If it's your drive to work every day, you know the exact route you'll take, and you don't need a map to guide you because you know the end from the beginning. If it's a first-time trip, you'll have a map or GPS to guide you so you know the destination. The same is true for your presentation."

"I can see the analogy apply in a number of ways."

"How?"

"Well, first, as the presenter, I need an outline that will work for me to serve as a reminder of the path I need to stay on while giving the presentation."

"Exactly, once you get comfortable with the presentation, it will be like driving to work. You'll be able to leave the map behind because you know the road."

"That's hard for me to imagine right now, but I'll trust you. Next, knowing the end from the beginning means I'm going to let the audience know the road we're taking and the destination."

Chloe interrupted, "That's so important. I know it's the age-old adage, but it's relevant today. Tell 'em what you're going to tell 'em; tell 'em; then, tell 'em what you told 'em. That's the essence of letting your audience know the direction and destination. Anything else?"

"There's more than one way to get to a destination, so I need to consider the different routes and be sure I choose one that fills the emotional fuel tank of the audience."

"That's really good," Chloe's energy nearly came through the computer screen. "Now, I've found one question that really helps me zero in on starting with the end in mind: what's the one thing I want a person in the audience to remember after they've left the room? When I answer that question, it gives me a distinct goal for the presentation."

"It's the thesis statement."

"Oh, my gosh!" Chloe exclaimed..

"What?" Mack asked.

"Thesis statement," Chloe said. "You said thesis statement, and that's dead on. It reminded me of a presentation I heard about a year ago from a local TV news anchor. She was speaking at a business luncheon about creating a thesis statement for your life. So much of what she said applied to giving presentations, too."

Mack asked, "Like what?"

"She started out talking about being a college student struggling to write a paper," Chloe began relaying the story. "When she called her dad to get some help in breaking through the writer's block, he asked her if she had written her thesis statement for the paper. Her dad was a teacher and was big on thesis statements. At first, she thought it was silly. But as soon as she developed the thesis statement, writing the paper became much easier." Chloe cocked her head to one side and checked Mack's image on her iPad screen, making sure he was still paying attention.

She continued, "The TV anchor then explained how the lack of a thesis statement in life can leave you with the equivalent of writer's block, not knowing how to get started or where to go. Then she explained how important it is to stay true to the thesis statement once you have it. She said it's really easy to get sidetracked and lose sight of your vision and mission."

Mack understood and picked up verbalizing the thought process. "So, if we apply the thesis statement principle to our presentation, we mustn't forget the destination, the goal of our presentation. People who relentlessly pursue their life's thesis statement aren't distracted. Presenters who relentlessly pursue the thesis statement aren't tempted to chase rabbit trails and get off topic, confusing the audience." He paused briefly, leaned in toward the camera on his laptop and said in a lower voice, "Presenters who relentlessly stick to the thesis statement are filling the fuel tank of each person in the audience because they exercise discipline and are working to do what's in the best interest of those with whom they are sharing."

"You're really picking up on this quickly," Chloe said.

BULLET POINTS

What's the one thing you want that person sitting on the back row to walk away from your presentation remembering? The question provides a key opportunity to develop your thesis statement, or in the infamous words of Curly Washburn played by Jack Palance in *City Slickers*, it's about one thing. What's your one thing? Don't deviate.

Screen time is so quickly diminishing your attention span; it's tough to capture your attention and hold it for any period. Think about yourself. How often are you compelled to check your phone for texts and e-mails? How often does your mind start to wander while listening to someone? Don't lie. Maintaining focus in the age of five-second sound bites, fifteen-second commercials, and no image lasting more than a few seconds on the TV, movie, or computer screen, which has so highly compressed our collective attention span, has made the presenter's job exponentially more difficult.

Are you able to change the attention span of each person in your audience or are you able to change your style to be more engaging? Both.

Both? you ask. Yes. You can influence the people in your audience by staying hyperfocused on the one message you want to convey. Remember, you must fill their emotional fuel tank. It's going to require you to constantly watch people in your audience for feedback and adjust accordingly. You'll see Mack watch for feedback in a common, but important, setting in the next chapter.

Bullet Point 11: As you create the road map (outline, text, bullet points, whatever you use) for your presentation, stay focused on the destination. Be dedicated.

ACTION

- Figure out a system to remind yourself to make important points and keep on track in your presentation. For some, it's an outline; for others, bullet points on index cards. Ultimately, get to a place where you're so practiced and prepared that you can give the presentation without looking at notes.

LAW OF PRESENTING: #6

Start with the end in mind.

Accomplish just one thing with each presentation, and do it well by staying focused on the destination.

8

THE SECOND SPEECH

"Luck favors the mind that is prepared."

—Louis Pasteur

Mack was grinning like the Cheshire Cat as he sat down to dinner with his family. Ellie hadn't seen this much joy on Mack's face in weeks. Mack passed the bowl of Pad Thai to Ellie. The family always made it a point to talk about the day's activities. It was a great time for Mack, Ellie, Devon, and Mikala to stay connected and discover what was going on in school, work, and life in general.

Ellie looked at Mack and said, "With a smile like that, I think you deserve to go first. What happened at work today?"

Barely unable to control his excitement, Mack began, "You wouldn't believe it! I gave a presentation today to the entire leadership team and knocked it out of the park." Mack paused to let the words sink in with those sitting around the table. Now, he definitely had everyone's attention.

"Well?" Ellie queried.

"I told you I had to give a presentation on a new technology we're deploying to improve communication with employees at all of InCirq's offices around the world. What would normally have been a ninety-minute aimless jumble of information, I condensed into twenty minutes and actually got a standing ovation."

"Honey, congratulations," she said. "We can see how excited you are, and we are so proud of you. But take it from the beginning. What happened?"

"I started with a story." Mack said. "We were in the conference room with the twenty-four people who lead the company. I started by saying, 'I want to tell you the story of an employee who thought he made a mistake but really created a new line of business for InCirq.' Everybody in the room snapped to attention. I told the story of Mike in R & D and how his discovery of the video chip led us to the place of developing a new piece of software. I shared the story of Abiah and how living out our values kept this top talent in InCirq and away from the competition. I just put the stories in a concise, linear format that was easy for people to understand. I explained that by living out the company's core values and relying on the people who are doing the work of making us one of the best chip makers in the world, we can do anything. No one can tell our story like we can, and if we don't communicate these successes and these lessons to all fifteen thousand employees, we won't create the culture we want to create."

Mack could tell he was starting to lose the kids with all of the business talk and knew that if he was going to make a habit of communicating and connecting with an audience, he had better engage Mikala and Devon.

"So Mikala," Mack said, "what's important for your cheer team? How do you look at a performance and know you were successful?"

"Somebody videos the cheers and then we watch to make sure everybody is doing it together."

"What if you did not have the video or a coach telling you what you were doing right?"

Mikala thought for a moment. "It would be really hard to get better."

"That's what we have to do at work," Mack explained. "We have to identify those things that people are doing right, watch for those things, tell people about those things, so that people know what to repeat."

Both kids nodded with understanding.

"Back to the story," Mack said, "I explained to the leadership team why we needed to give feedback on a more regular basis to the people who report to us—our employees. I had Mike demonstrate the new video streaming app, and it worked flawlessly because we had tested it over and over again before the actual presentation. As I closed the presentation, I told them we had the right people to develop the right technologies, and that it was our job to tell the stories, share the information, and encourage people. I laid out a challenge for each person on the leadership team to load the app on their phone by the end of the day, identify a person in the organization who is doing the right things, tell the story in a quick video chat just as I had done, and send the video to their direct reports. The apps would be installed on each employee's company-issued mobile device and computer in an overnight software update."

"Then why did you tell all the bosses to load the app if it was going to be done later?" Devon asked.

"Great question," Mack said. "You see, I asked the management team to load the app, first, because they have administrative clearance to manage apps on their devices, and second, I want them to feel ownership and understand how the technology works."

Ellie, Devon, and Mikala were genuinely happy for their dad. He'd never been so excited about giving a presentation.

Mack continued, "By the end of the day, eight people had loaded the app, and ten people e-mailed me to say it would be done within the next twenty-four hours." Mack had not taken a bite yet. He picked up a fork, tapped a tine on the plate next to his food, looked up to his family, and said, "I think that's the first time I've ever given a presentation and gotten an immediate response." Ellie started clapping and the two kids quickly joined in.

Later that night, with a glass of wine in hand, relaxing on the couch, Mack said to Ellie, "I'm excited to share the news with Chloe. I think she'll be impressed by the progress and success."

Ellie said, "Today was a big step for you. I can't tell you how impressed I am. I always knew it was in you. You just needed to tap the skills. Why don't you crack open your laptop and see if she's online?"

"You don't think it's too late?" Mack asked. The computer was on the floor leaning against the couch. Mack reached for it watching Ellie's reaction. She shook her head, no.

Mack opened Skype and looked to the list of contacts. Sure enough, Chloe was online. He hit the call button and after a few rings, the connection was live.

"Hey," Chloe said, "I was hoping you would call. I'm excited to hear an update. How did your presentation go today?"

"Are you sure it's not too late, and you have time for this?" Mack asked, watching closely for Chloe's reaction.

"No, all is good. I really want to hear," Chloe replied.

THE SECOND SPEECH

Mack told the story, just as he had recounted it for his family.

As he finished, Chloe interjected a question. "You sound like you really hit a stride and gained some confidence. What was the turning point? How did you calm yourself down and not let the stress sabotage the presentation?"

"That's hard for me to put my finger on it," Mack said, "but it started with the preparation. I literally drew a road map on the piece of paper, starting with the destination of launching a video app within the company. I worked back, highlighting the importance of our culture and core values, illustrating each point with a story."

"Great idea," Chloe said. "What else did you do to prepare?"

"I practiced it until I had the map memorized and knew each stop along the way," Mack said. "I have to tell you, in the moments leading up to the presentation, all those old feelings of, 'I'm going to bomb this speech,' came rushing back. For some reason, I thought back to playing high school football and something my coach told me, 'Five seconds at a time.'"

"Five seconds at a time?" Chloe asked.

"Yeah," Mack said. "Think about it. If you get so caught up in thinking about the whole game or entire presentation, it gets overwhelming, especially in the moments leading up to it. If it's the end of the third quarter of a football game and the starters are exhausted, thinking about playing an entire fourth quarter can be self-defeating. Instead, those players focus on one play at a time. On the presentation side, I ask myself all those self-defeating questions. Will I say anything that matters? Will I hold their attention for the full time? Will I lose my words halfway through? My coach explained the five-second philosophy as only focusing on giving it 100 percent for five-second bursts. Break it down into plays. I take the field and focus all of my attention on giving it my all for the five seconds of the play."

"But your presentation is longer than five seconds," Chloe said.

"I know," Mack said. "But the principle stays the same when I apply the idea to the road map. I quickly broke down the presentation into manageable bites and focused on each, giving 100 percent to each section, so I wouldn't get overwhelmed thinking about the entire presentation."

"I'd never thought of it like that before," Chloe said. "But I think you're onto something. It's the old adage: How do you eat an elephant? One bite at a time."

"That's it," Mack said. "It was really a breakthrough approach to keep me from burying myself in a pit of self-doubt."

"I'm very proud of you," Chloe paused and genuinely smiled. "Look, it's late. I have our next appointment scheduled with Mary. Enjoy the evening and I'll talk to you soon."

"Goodnight," Mack said. "Thank you, Chloe. You've been a huge help."

"You're welcome," she replied.

BULLET POINTS

Some professional speakers talk about spending several hours of preparation for each minute of the actual presentation. While that might not be a realistic expectation, you should be close to the hours-to-minutes equation. Take into account time spent in the shower ideating, time at the computer researching, and time in the car rehearsing. Preparation is key to success. Practice until you don't think you need to practice anymore. Then give the presentation one more run-through in your head. Preparation gives you confidence. Confidence helps you take your mind off yourself, so you can concentrate on what's most important. Remember, the presentation is for the audience.

Bullet Point 12: Preparation lays a foundation for success.

Manage your mind leading into the presentation by not getting overwhelmed with the entirety of the task at hand. Think, "bite-sized chunks." Then, give each section, each piece, each part, 100 percent effort.

ACTION

- Figure out the best way to lay out a road map for your preparation. Will it be bullet points, a graphical approach, an outline, or text of key points you need to make? Do what works for you, but make it easy for yourself to break the presentation into manageable pieces.

With all this said, you've truly arrived as an effective presenter when you can leave the notes behind and focus on having a quality conversation with the people who make up your audience (whether it's one, ten, one hundred, or one thousand).

9

CAUGHT OFF GUARD

""Be prepared for what?" someone once asked Robert Baden-Powell, the founder of Scouting.
"Why, for any old thing," said Baden-Powell.
—US Scouting Service Project

Mack felt a spring in his step as he walked into the InCirq management suite. He could feel a different energy. While he couldn't put his finger on it, Mack was sure the new energy was the result of his management team buzzing about the presentation three days ago. Each of the twenty-four had fully engaged, using the video app to send messages to their respective reports.

Mack approached Mary's desk, walking toward his office. "Good morning," she said. "I keep hearing people rave about your presentation. I wish I could have been in the room."

"Thank you," Mack said. "It was the first time I've ever felt good about giving a presentation."

Mary said, "Well, congratulations." Pausing just a moment and tapping her computer screen, she continued speaking. "You have a busy day. Remember there's a board meeting this afternoon."

"Yeah, I remember," Mack said. "I don't have any responsibility for the meeting. I'll just answer the standard questions."

"Okay," Mary said. "But remember, Norman will be in the meeting."

Mack stopped mid stride. "You know, Mary, I was having a really good day."

Emphasizing the word "was," a smile broke across his face. "Norman and I are just fine. He's very vocal and asks some good questions."

"He second-guesses everything you say and always has a better idea, at least if you ask him," Mary said, looking over her glasses at Mack.

"Like I said," Mack said in a reassuring voice. "All is well with Norman." He walked into his office.

As the clock struck 2:00 p.m., the board chair called the meeting to order. The group methodically made its way through the agenda. The fourteen people comprising the board sat in high-backed, black leather chairs around the massive mahogany conference room table.

Mack saw the meeting as an opportunity for his team to shine. As the chair made his way through the agenda, he called on individuals of the InCirq leadership group to provide quick reports, updating the board on a variety of initiatives. Norman always had a question or comment. Each person in the room had learned to expect it. Mack would interject bits and pieces of information if necessary but said very little at the meeting.

The group arrived at the last item on the agenda, and just as Mack started organizing the papers in front of him to prepare to leave the room, Norman said, "Mr. Chair, if I may, before we end the meeting, I have a question for Mack."

Mack felt the pressure resulting from stress start in his upper chest and quickly move up his neck into his head. He thought to himself, "Oh no, what now?"

The board chair gave permission to Norman to ask his question.

"Mack," Norman started. "I understand you're rolling out a video technology within the company. I'm having a really tough time understanding how this new initiative is within the scope of what InCirq is trying to accomplish." Norman looked around the room at the other board members, trying to make eye contact with each one, as though he was trying to rally support for his cause. He continued, "I think each one of us, as board members responsible for this company, deserve to see a pro forma business plan and know exactly what it is you want to accomplish with a video conferencing system. If we need it for an internal communication tool, why not buy it from a company that specializes in this type of technology? I just don't understand what you're trying to accomplish. Mr. Chair."

The chair looked at Mack, "Well, Mack. Care to respond?"

"Uh, um," Mack's head was swimming. He wasn't expecting to answer such questions. Norman's lengthy question, delivered more like a statement, provided just enough time for Mack's pituitary gland to go into action, sending the fight-or-flight chemical signal to his brain. Unknowingly, the chemical response inside Mack's body immediately caused his breathing to become shallow, starving his racing mind of oxygen, and setting in motion the downward spiral. A drop of perspiration formed just inside the hairline ahead of Mack's left temple. He felt it trickle down his cheek. Fractions of seconds felt like minutes as Mack inventoried his responses and the number of eyes directed at him. "I, I, well," he stammered.

Another bead of sweat formed and started to trickle down the right side of his forehead. "Do I draw more attention and wipe the sweat?"

Mack thought to himself. He could feel the moisture start to surface on the skin of his arms and back. His mouth, all of a sudden, went dry.

Using the back of his hand, Mack quickly wiped the top of his forehead.

"I, I, um," Mack was trying to force each word from his swirling mind to his uncooperative mouth. "I wasn't ready to share the video app with the board because it was so new, and . . ."

"That's not the point," Norman said. "I don't understand how development of a social media app is relevant to one of the largest chip-making companies in the world, trying to stay focused on being competitive in a cutthroat industry. It sounds to me like you're taking our eye off the game."

"No, I'm not taking our eye off the game," Mack said defensively. It was almost as though Norman was a circling shark, sensing blood in the water. "And, it's really not a social media . . ." Mack's voice immediately trailed off in unwitting deference to Norman.

"Well, Mack," Norman said, leaning forward and crossing his arms across his chest in an in-your-face way that said, *I dare you to prove me wrong.* "You tell me how taking precious company resources and redirecting the management team to make videos and asking employees to waste critical manufacturing time to watch the silly videos makes us more competitive."

Mack shifted in his seat, now, with small droplets of sweat reflecting the light originating from the lights in the conference room ceiling. In what felt like a last ditch effort to regain some semblance of composure, Mack again wiped his forehead with the back of his hand and said in a more forceful tone, "Listen, we wah…wah…want our people to innovate new ideas. I…I thought this, um, well, you know, it would improve, cuh…communication inside In-sir, um, the company and possibly, maybe, create a new stream of, muh, um, revenue."

Mack's mind raced through the numerous lessons learned with Chloe as he thought to himself, "Now I'm stuttering on top of everything else." No matter how hard he searched his memory, everything was a blur. Looking around the room, he could see sympathy on the faces of the other board members.

"Norman," InCirq's CEO, Steve Prichett interjected. "Obviously, Mack is not prepared to share with the board the new communication tool being tested. It's a small enough project, using such limited amounts of time and resources, that Mack has the freedom to experiment, and I haven't made the time to track it. We'll be sure to have a full explanation ready for you within a week, and we'll discuss it more during our next board meeting in a month."

"Thank you," Norman said, leaning back into his chair with a satisfied smirk on his face. "I think, as a board, it's our responsibility to keep you focused on the task at hand, and I see this as being a potential distraction, but I'd be happy to be proven wrong."

"Okay," the chair said, looking around the room. "Steve and Mack, if you'll get answers to Norman and the rest of the board within the week, that will be a help. Can I hear a motion to adjourn?"

Mack quickly made his way to a side exit door in the conference room and immediately went to his office. Barely five minutes had passed when Steve Prichett's head poked in his door. "What happened in there, Mack?" Steve asked. The two had known each other for years and worked well together. Steve had always known crowds and presenting made Mack incredibly nervous. He had placed Mack in the position of Chief Operating Officer because of Mack's skill and talent in monitoring InCirq's performance and recognizing opportunities before most senior executives he had worked with did during his thirty-five years of corporate experience. Steve had often thought that Mack's qualifications and track record overshadowed his fear of presenting.

"I'm really sorry, Steve," Mack said, shaking his head partly in disbelief at his performance and partly due to humiliation.

"I think it's a bit of a contradiction that you're creating a communication tool that has great potential, yet you have such a hard time communicating in front of a group. Do you think it's time to get some help in the area of making presentations?"

"Funny you'd say that," Mack responded. "I've been working with a person on my presentation skills. I thought I was making some real progress until today. I don't know what happened in there. I was taken completely off guard."

"Well, I'm glad to hear you're making progress," Steve said, "but you have some work to do to regain the confidence of the board after what just happened. Everyone in the company, including your team, realizes you know your stuff, but you need to remember the board doesn't interact with you on a day-to-day basis. The board will need a concise explanation of the video hardware and app. Can you put it together?"

"Absolutely," Mack said. "I'll have it ready this week."

"Okay," Steve said, tapping the door frame twice with his hand as he turned to leave.

BULLET POINTS

Ouch! Getting caught off guard is a horribly uncomfortable place to be as a presenter. That's why thinking ahead and anticipating the tough questions are so important. Norman is a known commodity. Everyone expects him to ask the tough questions and make statements for the sake of making statements. I'm sure you know someone who likes to talk, and often bully, just to exert force. Call it the alpha dog syndrome. This aggressive, hard-driving person is basically doing the equivalent of marking territory. It's just what the alpha dog will do, given the chance and a nearby fire hydrant.

Don't even waste time thinking you can change people who act like the alpha dog, exerting psychological force to reinforce a position of power. It's better to be prepared to navigate around such people.

If dealing with such people is a major obstacle (more than we're able to deal with in this book), I recommend you read *Crucial Conversations and Crucial Confrontations* by the author team of Kerry Patterson, Joseph Grenny, David Maxfield, Ron McMillan, and Al Switzler.

More than anything, the lesson from this chapter is to go into any setting prepared. Think, Boy Scout.

Mack knew Norman's reputation. What if Mack would have called Norman on the phone within a few days of the meeting to ask if Norman had any questions he would like addressed at the meeting? Imagine if Mack would have made the phone call and said, "Norman, you ask the good questions that make people think and keep us focused on InCirq's future. Do you have any questions you want answered at the board meeting? If I know now, I can be prepared."

I learned this technique, called "the meeting before the meeting," from John Maxwell. In a message about lessons learned as a young pastor, Maxwell relayed the story of a challenging church board member. Maxwell would make it a point to speak with the board member before each meeting—sharing ideas, asking for input, asking for questions and concerns—having the meeting before the meeting.

> **Bullet Point 13: The meeting before the meeting is an effective way to think about your audience first. You're preparing, connecting ahead of time, seeking clarity, and paving the way for effective, efficient communication.**

Don't wait on the person you perceive as a challenge to take the initiative to work with you. Make the first step and initiate the conversation, seeking clarity for all involved in the sharing of information. A byproduct of good preparation is stress reduction.

How do you control the physiological reaction to stress?

First, be aware. If you know you perspire in tense situations, keep a handkerchief in a pocket so you can wipe your brow. Wear a dark suit jacket when presenting to hide armpit perspiration. While you can experiment with different brands and types of antiperspirants, there are some physical reactions to stress that won't be stopped. You need to figure out a way to compensate, downplay, or hide the negative responses.

Shallow breathing is one of the first indications of a downward spiral. It reduces the amount of oxygen in your blood stream. Your brain needs highly oxygenated blood to operate at peak performance. Shallow breathing makes speaking much more difficult. A shallow breath leaves you stuttering and stammering trying to get enough air to speak a complete sentence without stopping midstream to take a breath.

ACTION

- Create a habit of breathing deeply by focusing on breathing air deep enough into your lungs to see your stomach expand with each inhale.

Deep breathing provides your brain with oxygen, gives your lungs the air needed to speak in complete sentences, and ultimately, goes a long way toward calming your nerves. What's the first thing you say to a child who is visibly upset, crying, and trying to grasp a breath of air? You most likely say (in a calm, soothing voice), "Take a deep breath." The advice worked then and it works now. Take a deep breath.

Once you recognize your physiological responses to stress, embrace them. It might be hard to imagine those responses as positive now, but keep telling yourself: "This is me. I'm going to do and be the best with what I have." Feed on that nervous energy. Channel the energy to help you give the audience the best of you.

10

REBUILD

"Spontaneity is conditioned reflex."
—Denis Waitley, *The Psychology of Winning*

"I'm so sorry," Chloe said genuinely, as Mack finished telling the story of yesterday's board meeting.

"The past is the past," she continued. "Your CEO, Steve, was right on when he said you have some work to do in rebuilding the confidence of the board. So, since the past is the past, what are you going to do now?"

"I'm going to answer the questions," Mack said. "Showing how the video hardware and app are within the scope of what we do and will help us improve internal processes so that we can be more competitive."

Chloe and Mack were sitting across from one another at the same conference room table where Mack had bumbled his way through answering Norman's question less than twenty-four hours earlier.

"Can you meet the deadline?" Chloe asked.

"You know," Mack said. "Within ten minutes of leaving the meeting, I had formulated all the answers to the questions in my mind. I immediately put it on paper, and now I'm running it by Steve before I forward it to Norman."

Chloe said, "Then, the big question is, how do you keep this from happening again?"

"My wife gave me a great idea to answer your big question," Mack said.

"Really?" Chloe said, leaning forward with her hands on top of the table. "Do share."

"She asked me if I would consider calling Norman a day or two ahead of the next meeting and giving him an honest compliment," Mack said rolling his eyes. "That might be a little tough, but I think I can do it. Then, I share with him anything I'm working on that would reach board-level concern, and then ask if he has any other questions, so I can be fully prepared for our next meeting."

"That's fabulous advice, Mack," Chloe said. "You're having the meeting before the meeting."

"Yep," Mack said while raising an eyebrow with a slight smile of satisfaction in realizing the power of such a simple step.

"I've been there," Chloe said. "Being caught off guard in front of a group of people—it's not fun. But, it sounds like you've already done what you need to move on. The important piece is rebuilding your confidence so yesterday's event doesn't have a chance to replay in your mind the next time you have the opportunity to present in front of a group. Just thinking about it can set you back."

"What happened to you?" Mack asked, nearly in disbelief that Chloe would have suffered a similar communication implosion.

"It was just a couple years ago," she began telling the story. "I thought I was just going to coffee with a small group of people to talk about a new app development company I was putting together with some friends. It turned out a potential investor was joining us, and in the rush of putting the coffee together, I and another partner were never told who was joining us or why. The guy started peppering us with questions that I wasn't prepared to answer." Chloe paused just a moment, thinking back to the scene of her and five other people sitting around a white, laminate-covered table in the simple, but trendy coffee shop.

"So, what did you do?" Mack asked.

"I stumbled and bumbled my way through a convoluted and confusing answer, made up an excuse that I needed to leave, and on my way out the door vowed to never let that happen again."

"I'll bet you let your friends have it when you saw them again," Mack said with a smile.

"No," Chloe said somberly. "I'm a big believer in personal responsibility. We are where we are in life solely due to the choices we make. I blame no one. I made a choice to attend that meeting without asking the simplest of questions: Who else is going to be there? What will we be talking about? Is there anything I can do ahead of time to be fully prepared?"

"You're right," Mack said thoughtfully. "When you say it like that, it was definitely my responsibility to be ready for yesterday's meeting and I wasn't."

"Recognizing the problem is the first step," Chloe said, smiling to break the somber attitude. "Let's spend today's time figuring out how to prepare for anything."

"Obviously, the first step is to ask for the meeting before the meeting," Mack said. "But what if a meeting before the meeting is not possible?"

"Practice," Chloe said matter-of-factly.

Mack scrunched up his face in a look of confusion. "What do you mean?" he asked.

"I'll illustrate it with a story," Chloe said. "I really enjoy being around high school kids. Their energy and attitude, I just think it's an interesting phase in life. I had a friend who was a principal at a high school. I asked her about opportunities to get involved in the school. She explained that she could bring instructors into the school to teach specialized subjects as long as the instructor had a level of education and experience equipping them to teach the class. I asked if it were possible for me to teach such a class. We batted around some ideas and settled on innovative thinking for the advanced students. I'd studied it extensively in my master's program and had continued to stay current by reading the latest works by thought leaders. The principal asked me to put together a course syllabus.

That was July. By the end of August, I was teaching a 7:30 a.m. elective class to twenty high school seniors. I was scared to death about the prospect. How was I going to capture the attention of those kids and keep them engaged? It is the challenge we all face as presenters. I approached the idea of teaching the class by following all the concepts we've been discussing. I custom tailored the course material, found ways to make it relevant to the kids in the room, and stayed focused on keeping the end in mind. I basically made a daily seventy-minute presentation on innovative thinking."

"Wow," Mack said. "Impressive. But I'm not able to go out and teach a high school class."

"That's not the point," Chloe said. "The biggest lesson I learned was to treat every communication opportunity as a chance to hone my skills, because what I learned in the classroom transferred to everything else I did. I learned how to engage the audience, check for understanding, make people feel ownership, and discover new ways to create relevance. It wasn't about teaching a class; it was about communicating and the realization that we do it all the time. Do I take those daily interactions with family, friends, and coworkers for granted; or do I treat those occurrences like practice by always trying to improve my communication? Teaching the class taught me to choose the latter. Every time I engage with people there's usually something to learn. How can I be a better listener? How can I be clearer? How can I first seek to understand before trying to be understood?"

"Okay," Mack said, "I get it. It's like that quote I saw somewhere, 'spontaneity is conditioned reflex.' I make good communication a habit by treating every communication opportunity as a chance to improve my skills."

"There you go," Chloe said. "It's taking advantage of what you already do, but being more strategic about your approach."

BULLET POINTS

The opening exchange between Chloe and Mack presents the classic response pattern to address any crisis. Mack found himself in a self-caused crisis. He took action immediately to recognize and own the problem. He instantly went to work fixing the problem and then, finally, started finding a way to keep the problem from happening again.

> **Bullet Point 14: Three steps to crisis communication: (1) own it, (2) fix it, and (3) prevent it from happening again.**

Communicating through and immediately after a crisis is a crucial opportunity that cannot be squandered. It has been famously said, never let a crisis go to waste. You can take the negative approach and use a crisis for political gain to the detriment of your reputation and level of trust others have in you. The alternative would be to go to the positive, and use the crisis as an opportunity to show responsibility, clarity, and the ability to learn, grow, and improve. Which do you choose?

You've no doubt heard the phrase, practice makes perfect. You've also probably heard the rebuttal, perfect practice makes perfect. The only way to get better at presenting is to practice. You might not have the opportunity to teach a daily class, but unless you're a hermit living alone on the side of a mountain, you're engaging in daily communication by sharing information with others. Use those daily interactions as the perfect practice that leads to improvement. Focus on one area of improvement per day.

ACTION

- Create a perfect practice strategy to improve your communication skills.

For example, Mondays are your days to focus on the tried-and-true concept of seek first to understand before being understood. Think empathy. This is a must-have listening skill. If you don't quite understand the concept, learn about emotional intelligence (EI) and your aptitude to relate to others. (We'll touch a bit more EI in the Bullet Points from chapter 14.)

Tuesdays can be your days to record your side of the conversation while speaking on the phone, listening for annoying verbal habits. Use the voice memo app on your smartphone or a digital audio recorder to record while you are speaking. Play it back, listening for the number of times you use uh, um, you know, like . . . and the list of crutch words goes on. Create a mental checklist to eliminate the unnecessary words.

On Wednesdays, check for understanding. Make a conscious effort to watch the reactions of those around you. Are people glazing over when you speak? Is there a look of confusion? Watch for understanding and adjust your communication to increase the level of audience comprehension.

Thursdays are put-people-first days. Think, "First Thursday." Get yourself in the habit of putting the audience first, remembering that little things matter. Open doors for others. Encourage others to go first. Give up your place in the grocery store checkout line to the person who walked up behind you with only two items. No matter the setting, find ways to put people first. This simple act is a servant leadership principle; really, it's a leadership law. John Maxwell wrote in his online leadership guide, *Unplugged*:

> Servant leadership should be a way of life for all of us. The essence of servant leadership is valuing people and adding value to their lives. If you value people, you want to serve. If you devalue people, you want to be served. Maturity is the ability to think of others first.

Designate one day a week to work on complete sentences. Call it speaking in sound bites. Put every thought into a complete sentence in your brain before speaking it. It's going to feel clumsy at first. However, this perfect practice technique will create a habit in your brain to formulate the complete sentences before speaking. It eliminates crutch words and run-on sentences.

ACTION

- One of the best ways to improve your ability to speak in complete sound bites is to read. Read fiction. Read nonfiction. Read blogs. Read the newspaper. Follow thought-provoking people on Twitter or through an RSS feed, a way many news-related sites and blogs deliver regularly changing web content. Whatever you enjoy reading, read it more. Set aside time each day to read.

11

WORD PICTURES

*"Stories are attempts to share our values and beliefs.
Storytelling is only worthwhile when it tells
what we stand for, not what we do."*
—Simon Sinek

Watching The Weather Channel was one of Mack's funny little quirks. At least, that's what Ellie thought. Mack thought it was a perfectly rational thing to do. With as little time as he spent in front of the television, he often found himself watching the network known for all things meteorological. This night was no different. The house was empty, except for Mack, who was sitting on the couch. Ellie was at dinner with a group of friends, Devon was in the middle of an evening lacrosse clinic, and Mikala was at a friend's home. Mack had settled in his favorite spot, the corner of the living room sectional. The TV was turned on to The Weather Channel, and his iPad rested on a pillow on his lap as he reviewed month-end financials. Mack wasn't paying close attention to the documentary about hurricanes.

Another commercial break, while Mack furrowed his eyebrows, trying to remember why line fifty-six, administrative office supplies, showed an actual number that was higher than budgeted. He touched his finger to the screen and pulled up a detailed expense report for the line item. "Oh, that's it," he thought to himself glancing up at the TV. The hurricane documentary had returned and the image on the screen was of a large, four-engine prop airplane with a giant disc mounted under its belly. Mack turned up the volume out of curiosity. The narrator explained the P3 Turboprop was flown into the eye of the hurricane to record data. The pilot of the plane was being interviewed.

"It's kinda like driving an eighteen-wheeler," NOAA Pilot, Commander Phil Kenul said as he appeared on screen, "with a couple flat tires, bad suspension, potholed road, ninety miles an hour without any headlights at midnight. That gives you an idea. Mix that up with a really bad elevator ride, and you know what it can be like."

"That's it," Mack thought to himself. "That's what Chloe was talking about when she told me I needed to be thinking about using word pictures when telling stories." Mack made a mental note to share the story with Chloe at their scheduled Skype conference in just over an hour. Right on time, Ellie and Devon walked in the door.

Chloe sat in her hotel room, a two-hour time difference separating her and Mack as the two conversed via Skype. Her e-mail to him earlier in the week had been titled, "Word Pictures." She had told him to start thinking more strategically about how he told stories. Word pictures were a terrific way to help people experience the story he was sharing. When he initially read the e-mail, he wasn't quite sure how to incorporate word pictures into his stories. Watching The Weather Channel hurricane documentary earlier had lit the proverbial light bulb above his head. He immediately told Chloe the story of the pilot explaining the feeling of flying the plane.

"Let's watch it," Chloe said. "I'm going to share my screen and do a quick YouTube search for the video." Within moments, Chloe found the video. It began to play. Mack smiled as he watched Chloe react to the pilot's words.

WORD PICTURES

"So," Mack asked when the video was over. "Is that what you mean when you say, 'Use word pictures'?"

"That's exactly it. Do you *see* what he's doing?"

"I do. Word pictures make perfect sense."

"Do you have any experience flying a plane or do you know any pilots?"

"I took a few hours of lessons and spent some time flying with pilot friends."

"They speak a whole different language, don't they? Setting the trim, attitude, rudders, stabilizers."

"Yeah. They can definitely be hard to understand."

"But not that pilot," Chloe said. "Instead of talking about technical airplane terms, he used descriptive words that just about anyone can relate to and understand. Who hasn't driven on a road full of potholes? Bad elevator rides are memorable. All those quick descriptors helped a diverse audience—the people watching a Weather Channel documentary—really understand what it feels like to be in the cockpit of that airplane. You found a great example of word pictures done well."

"I really understand the relevance piece now," Mack said. "I have friends who fly, and I get so frustrated listening to them use acronyms and talk airplane lingo; I thought the pilot on TV was much easier to understand."

"What are some other ways you can use word pictures?" Chloe asked.

"You mean in my presentations?" Mack responded back with a question.

"Yes," Chloe said. "In your presentation or in everyday conversation."

"Rather than just reading off reams of numbers when talking about data and providing reports, I can illustrate specific numbers with a story or analogy that a lot of people can relate to. Let's see." Mack rubbed his chin, thinking about an example. "So, I was going through our financials earlier tonight and realized we were over budget on the expense line for administrative office supplies. I could go in and tell my team that we're over budget by nearly $7,000, or I could spend a little time developing the analogy that our administrative department bought enough toner to fill 100 gallon-size milk jugs. Being $7,000 over budget on expenses is the equivalent of blowing our family's food budget on eating out at restaurants ten nights out of the month at $60 a pop.

"Excellent example," Chloe broke in with a smile. "Obviously, when delivering news like that, it's all in the delivery. Be sure you have high levels of trust and you're communicating in the same room, so they can see all of your nonverbal communication at play."

Mack chuckled, "Yeah, I wouldn't write that one in an e-mail."

"As you can tell," Chloe said, "word pictures take work, but the impact on your audience is tremendous. I think you'll find it's worth the time and effort."

Mack and Chloe wrapped up the conversation with Chloe explaining she would connect with Mary and set the date for their next conversation. Just as Chloe was about to hit the red hang-up button, Mack said, "Oh, hold on. I almost forgot."

"What's up?" Chloe asked.

"I'm being called in to a board committee meeting tomorrow. Norman will be there. Could we spend about five minutes war gaming?"

Chloe unconsciously glanced at the upper right corner of her computer screen to check the time. It was two hours later thanks to the time zone difference. "Sure," she said with a genuine smile. "I'm glad you brought it up. I've been meaning to share a document I use to help prepare for tough conversations. Hold on, one second." She paused between words as Mack watched her eyes race across the screen as she opened folders, opened her e-mail, copied and pasted a file, and hit send. She said, "There. You should have that attachment in a few seconds.

"That was fast," Mack said moments later. "I have it." Double clicking on the file, the document opened on Mack's iPad screen. "It's a table," he said matter-of-factly, almost with a hint of disappointment.

"I know," Chloe said. "It's actually what I call a message map. The words you will put into that table are important. See there across the top, there's one empty box that stretches across the top of the three-column, three-row table?"

Mack nodded his head as he stared intently at his tablet screen.

Topic, reason for conversation, "thesis statement"		
Column 1: First key concept	Column 2: Second key concept	Column 3: Third key concept
A. Supporting thought, statement or story	A. Supporting thought, statement or story	A. Supporting thought, statement or story
B. Supporting thought, statement or story	B. Supporting thought, statement or story	B. Supporting thought, statement or story
C. Supporting thought, statement or story	C. Supporting thought, statement or story	C. Supporting thought, statement or story

Chloe continued, "That's the headline box. Type the objective of the meeting. What do you want to accomplish? Then, you'll see that the top row is the column header row. The top row in the first column is one, the second column is two, and the top row of the third column is three. Those are the boxes you write the key message or, in the case of preparing for Norman, this is where you anticipate the questions he'll ask related to the meeting. You'll work to develop answers to those questions in the column boxes under each row header, labeled A, B, and C. It sounds complicated, but let's work through the questions first."

"No, no, I see it," Mack said nodding his head up and down as he continued looking at the blank table on his screen. He started typing as he spoke. "So, the top line is going to say, hmmm," he paused. "Do I put the subject of the meeting or the reason I'm creating the message map?"

"That's the beautiful thing about the message map," Chloe said. "It's exactly what you need it to be. You could actually create one for the meeting and one for what you need to anticipate from Norman." Chloe stopped, furrowed an eyebrow, and leaned in toward the camera. "You did have the meeting before the meeting with Norman, didn't you?"

Mack chuckled, "Yes, I called him on the phone today."

"Great," Chloe said. "Had to check. What did he say?"

"He's still not convinced the video hardware and app are the right direction for InCirq," Mack said.

"Okay," Chloe said. "Then let's create the message map to address his concerns."

Mack started typing and talking, "Video hardware and app, mission-driven for InCirq. Okay, the top line is filled in."

"Now, let's start with column A," Chloe said. "You can think of it this way: what are the top three reasons the video hardware and app align with the mission? Write each of those reasons in boxes A, B, and C."

Mack stared at his screen. "Yes," he said. "I completely see how this is going to work. I'd like a little time to put some thought into it."

Chloe said, "So, you see that your supporting word picture, thoughts, and examples fill in the boxes for each reason in boxes A, B, and C?"

"I do see it," Mack said. "We've talked in the past about creating a road map. This looks like a great tool to keep me focused on the message."

"Hence, the message map," Chloe said. "Go ahead, spend some time plugging ideas into each of the boxes on the table, then feel free to e-mail it to me if you have questions or would like some feedback."

"Perfect," Mack said. "Thank you so much for taking a few extra minutes."

BULLET POINTS

Anyone can throw a PowerPoint slide of numbers, charts, and graphs on the wall. Truly skilled communicators turn the material into a story that people in the audience can visualize without the help of a computer screen-projected image on the wall.

Albeit, storytelling takes a lot of work, especially when you consider the alternative of putting a spreadsheet in front of your audience and saying, "Here are the numbers, facts, or figures." The questions to keep at the forefront of your mind: what's the value of my time and what's the collective value of time for those in the audience?

When you answer these questions honestly, you have no other option than to invest the time in becoming a skilled storyteller. The skill is evident in your ability to use word pictures to activate the imagination of each person in the audience.

Now, don't freak out about having to use word pictures as you tell stories. It's part of your genetic code. People have told stories since the beginning of time. Scratchings on cave walls to the art of oral history to the Dr. Seuss books you grew up with and read to your kids—stories are a part of who we are as a civilization. Rather than work so hard to eliminate stories from the lexicon of business, why not embrace stories to increase understanding, retention, and impact of the information you share?

Bullet Point 15: Great stories have three things in common: challenge, struggle, and resolution (CSR).

Apply the CSR test to your stories. Present the challenge by setting up the protagonist and antagonist. Always remember that there is honor in the struggle, and people appreciate and cheer for the underdog. Finally, we find inspiration in the win. Wins are memorable. Do you remember being a part of a winning team? How did it make you feel? Good, right? Ah, now you see, we start filling the emotional fuel tank when we present the CSR in a way that is relevant to the audience, helping people relate and engage.

ACTION

- Practice using word pictures when telling stories at home around the dinner table. Rather than saying, "My day was okay," be prepared to share a specific story about identifying a challenge, struggling through the process, and finding resolution. Try to bring the story to life for those sitting around the table. Practice your storytelling skills so it becomes second nature.

12

CRUCIAL MEETING

*"Gratitude is when memory is stored in the heart
and not in the mind."*
—Lionel Hampton

Message map in hand, Mack was in the boardroom, waiting for committee members to arrive for the meeting. He had polished his message on the folded piece of paper, shared it with Chloe, and received her feedback. No doubt about it, he was ready.

Within minutes, the six committee members entered the room and sat around the table. The committee chair called the meeting to order, put his hand on the piece of paper laying on the table that served as the meeting agenda, let his finger go to the item listed number one, and said, "Let's get started with the agenda."

Norman had requested the committee meeting after receiving the answers to his questions about the video hardware and app.

"Mack," the chair said. "Let's start with you and a quick explanation of what InCirq is working to accomplish with the video chip combination and app."

"I'd be happy to," Mack said. "You've all heard the story of our R & D engineer, Mike, who accidentally discovered how well our existing chip worked with the HD video component from our partner in Asia. We have a good track record of success in developing apps that make full use of our hardware. The two teams, R & D and the app developers, collaborated to find an innovative use for the hardware combination." Mack stopped to check for understanding on the faces in the room. Each person was leaning forward, intently listening, except for one. Norman, his arms crossed, leaned back in his chair.

Mack had committed the message map to memory. It was an easy process because of the simplicity of the format. "There are three ways I see the technology helping InCirq," Mack continued. "First, we arrived at this place by following our values of putting people first. The story of Mike in R & D shows we have employees dedicated to pushing the envelope, moving us forward with new and unique ideas. We listened to him and gave him a chance. The way we should see it, as leaders, we need to encourage new ideas by providing opportunities to investigate, learn, and fail. Our approach inspires others on the team to be courageous in exploring new ways for InCirq to continue dominating the market."

Mack paused briefly to take a sip of water. As he put the drinking glass back on the table, he said, "Second on the list, it falls within the mission of the organization." Mack looked at Norman with a knowing hint of a smile. The two had spent nearly an hour on the phone the day before, working through Norman's concerns. "And it's here I need to pause and say thank you to Norman for keeping us on track and focused on what matters most. He asked the right questions during the board meeting. The two of us had a good conversation yesterday. He's doing the work of a good, fiscally responsible board member."

Without thinking, Norman smiled, uncrossed his arms, straightened in his chair and leaned forward.

"Norman and I have identified a few ways the project achieves mission for InCirq," Mack continued. "First, the heart of the technology is InCirq's proprietary chipset. The system doesn't work without our chip. We actually tested the camera connected to our competitor's chips of similar design and use, and the system didn't work. We couldn't replicate the success we found with our chip. So, second, we have an opportunity to create new market share. If you've read the book *Blue Ocean Strategy* by W. Chan Kim and Renee Mauborgne, we're in the uncluttered, calm waters of our niche, not the shark-infested competitive waters where other chip companies are operating."

Mack noticed two of the committee members writing the book title on notepaper provided to each person. "And third," Mack said. "We accomplish our mission by creating a new revenue stream. We've already run the numbers. A simplified version of the app can be offered for free with a robust, full version offered for a one-time fee of $19.99. Conservative projections indicate ten million units will be sold in the United States within the first year. Because of the unique combination of the camera and chip, our partner tells us they have a significant competitive advantage in negotiations to place the technology in multiple brands of smartphones and tablets."

At this revelation, smiles broke out on the faces of each of the six people sitting around the table. Mack was on a roll and he could feel the momentum building as he worked through the message map. Visualizing the third column in his mind, he forged ahead. "Finally, this technology will save InCirq at least $50,000 this year, while increasing our ability to communicate with the fifteen thousand people who work for the company."

Mack summarized executive travel savings realized by using the video sharing app, explained the interactive push technology behind the app and its ability to engage users, and that 97 percent of InCirq employees used a smartphone or tablet on a daily basis. "It all adds up to an opportunity for us to engage the great people at InCirq, further our mission, and become more cost efficient and productive," Mack said, providing a one-sentence sound bite to summarize the message map.

The committee chair asked for questions and after a few congratulatory statements from those sitting around the table, continued with the agenda.

Later that day, Mack opened his laptop and noticed he'd left Skype open from the night before. He glanced at the contact list and saw the green cloud icon with a check mark inside next to Chloe's name. "Let's see if she'll answer," Mack thought to himself as he clicked the call button. After a couple rings, he saw her image appear on his screen. "Do you have a moment?" Mack asked.

"Sure," Chloe said. "How did the meeting go?"

"That's why I'm calling," Mack said. "It was amazing. The message map worked like a charm. I felt prepared and ready for anything. I had to call to say thank you."

"You're welcome," Chloe responded. "What about Norman?"

"The meeting before the meeting has completely turned him around," Mack said. "After I recognized him in today's meeting and was sincerely grateful for the questions he asked earlier, it felt like he was cheering me on. It's a complete change."

Chloe said, "That's fantastic. Congratulations."

"Hey," Mack said. "I couldn't have done it without you. Thanks, and I see you're at your typical office. Enjoy a cup of coffee for me."

"Yep, you know you can usually find me at a coffee shop," Chloe said, raising her white paper cup within site of the camera embedded in the top of her laptop screen. "Cheers to you."

"Cheers," Mack said. "I'll talk to you soon."

BULLET POINTS

David Horsager, author of *The Trust Edge*, said, "There are people who walk into a room and light it up, and there are people who walk out of a room and light it up." The audience laughed when he said it in reference to magnetic traits. Once again, we're talking about filling the emotional fuel tank of those in the audience. Gratitude is one of the most magnetic traits. Sincere gratitude works every time. Would you rather be around someone who is thankful or complains? Probably the former. What type of person are you? Presenters who grasp the gravity of gratitude connect with their audience at a deeper level.

By the way, you can't fake gratitude and get away with it. People will see through you and you'll lose credibility. Thankfulness must be true and genuine. Horsager wrote in his book, "People who learn to be thankful are more content and fulfilled. The single greatest commonality of happy people is an attitude of gratitude, people find it attractive."

Find opportunities to express real gratitude to individuals and groups as you present. The attitude of gratitude makes you attractive to your audience.

ACTION

- Name four to five things you're grateful for. Inventory your thank-you list. Make gratefulness a daily habit so it shows in your presentation style.

As you develop your message map, it's important you commit the concepts to memory and not read the paper. Remember, you are the expert or at least the most knowledgeable person to speak on the topic at this place and time. Reading your statement from a message map is not genuine and creates the impression you are not prepared or you don't know the material. Commit the concepts listed on the message map to memory.

Bullet Point 16: Humbly share your knowledge with others.

As you seek wisdom, you can add value to people by humbly sharing what you know and where you learned it. In fact, when you find a really good book, buy an extra copy and share it along with a personalized note. Trinkets, pen sets, and logo-labeled anything quickly collect dust, break, wear out, or get lost. Wisdom and knowledge shared in the form of a book can never be lost, broken, or stolen once read.

LAW OF PRESENTING: #7

Be grateful.

An attitude of genuine gratitude is appealing. Thankfulness is attractive. Wear it often.

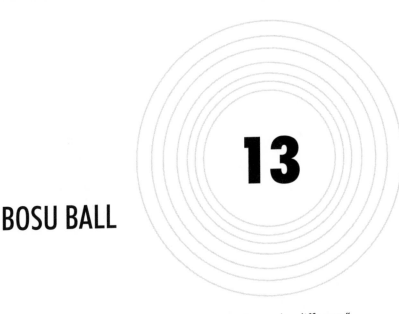

13

BOSU BALL

"In order to be irreplaceable, one must always be different."
—Coco Chanel

As planned, Mack arrived at the gym at 4:00 p.m. on Thursday to meet Chloe. Earlier in the week when he asked what she had in mind, she said, "Trust me." He'd learned enough up to this point to do just that.

Mack walked through the front doors and into an open entry with high ceilings, a tile floor, and a young woman behind the waist-high black granite counter whose smile and enthusiasm left Mack with nothing to do but smile as he walked up to the desk. She asked, "How can I help you?"

"I'm supposed to meet Chloe." The woman cut him off before he could say Chloe's last name.

"Oh yeah," she said. "You're Mack. Welcome! Chloe left a visitor pass with me, so you're good to go. She's in fitness Studio C. Just walk down this hall," she said, pointing past the reception counter down a long, wide hallway. "Walk past the pool and basketball courts. You'll turn left just after the locker rooms and you'll see the first door on your right is Studio C."

"Thank you," Mack said as he started walking past the reception desk.

Mack quickly found the door marked Studio C and opened it. The space was large but much darker than the rest of the gym. Mack immediately noticed the almost red hardwood floors with black mats spaced evenly throughout. In the middle of the room were what appeared to be exercise balls sunk into the floor. The room was also much warmer. Chloe was next to a mirrored wall, talking to another woman. She noticed Mack as soon as he walked in and said, "Excuse me," to the woman and jogged over to Mack. "Good afternoon," she said, extending her hand to shake Mack's.

Mack said, "If I didn't know better, I'd think you have plans for me to do yoga."

"Oh no," Chloe replied. "I told you to trust me. Meet Rebecca," she said motioning to the woman to join her and Mack. Rebecca walked quickly up to Mack, extending her hand to shake his.

"Good to meet you, Rebecca," Mack said, returning the handshake.

Chloe continued, "Rebecca is a yoga instructor, but her class doesn't start until five, so I asked her if she could help me demonstrate the Bosu Ball."

"Is that what those are?" Mack asked, pointing to the two exercise balls he'd noticed when he walked into the room.

"Yeah," Rebecca said as she started walking toward the center of the room. "Come on over and get barefoot." Mack did as instructed, removing his shoes and socks. He was somewhat athletic, playing golf and tennis, but the idea of exercising in a warm, dark room on a

BOSU BALL

Bosu Ball didn't sound like much fun. The balls were arranged about five feet from one another. Rebecca stepped up on the ball with her feet together, quickly balancing herself.

"Go ahead and take a wide stance, standing on the ball," Rebecca said as she spread her feet apart, demonstrating the instructions.

Mack instinctively put his hands out for balance as he stepped up onto the ball. He found his balance faster than he expected.

Chloe was standing off to the side watching Mack. She noticed the look of relief on his face. "It was a little easier than you expected, right?"

"I was expecting it to be much more difficult," Mack said.

"Mack," Rebecca said. "I want you to slowly turn to face me. Now, reach out and grab my hands so we can lean on each other."

The balls were placed far enough apart that each person would have to lean toward the other in order to clasp hands. Mack immediately got a little wobbly as he placed himself in the position Rebecca had directed. Once again, Mack was surprised at the ease with which he accomplished the task.

"Tell me what you are experiencing," Rebecca said.

"I, um, well," Mack stammered, not sure exactly what to say. "I was a bit suspicious of what you were going to have me do, but I'm finding it pretty easy. When you asked me to lean in toward you, I got really nervous, but I actually regained my balance even more quickly than when I first stepped onto the ball. Now that I have someone to lean against, my balance is even better."

"Good observation," Rebecca said, looking at Chloe with a knowing smile on her face. "Did we accomplish what you wanted?"

"Yep," Chloe said with a beaming smile. "It's time for an iced tea. Come on, Mack," she said as Rebecca gently pushed Mack back toward an upright position.

"Wait," Mack said. "That's it? That wasn't a workout. I didn't even break a sweat."

Chloe said, "It wasn't supposed to be a work out. I'll explain. Thank you, Rebecca. I might be a few minutes late for class, but I'll be back." Chloe and Mack made their way to the front of the gym where a food bar was set up. Mack hadn't noticed it when he first walked into the gym.

With hands wrapped around their clear plastic cups of iced tea, Chloe and Mack sat on stools at a high table nearest the entry to the gym.

"That was a bit strange," Mack said. "What exactly was I supposed to learn from that?"

Chloe said, "Every time I start a presentation, I think of each person in the audience standing on a Bosu Ball, just like you were standing on the Bosu Ball. How did you describe it?"

"At first, I was suspicious," Mack said.

"Exactly," Chloe said. "Isn't that how you often feel when you're in the audience and hearing someone present for the first time?" Without waiting for an answer, Chloe continued. "If we continually think audience first, we need to realize the audience is going to be a bit suspicious of you, the presenter, in the beginning. You'll have some people who will sit there, leaning back in the chair with arms crossed with that look of, 'Tell me something I don't know; I dare you.' You'll have others who have been through enough mind-numbing sales pitches, PowerPoint presentations, and monotonous sales training that they'll just sit there with a blank stare. Each person in the audience is trying to figure out their balance on the make-believe Bosu Ball."

"Mmmm," Mack murmured thoughtfully as he sipped his tea and contemplated the analogy.

Chloe continued, "Then, almost immediately, Rebecca took you off balance again. Think of Rebecca as the presenter. She changed your paradigm and gave you the tools to quickly regain your balance and be more comfortable. Right?"

"Yeah, absolutely," Mack said, taking another sip of tea. "I was snapped out my newfound comfort zone, and I briefly lost balance while turning on the ball. But I soon found myself in a better place of balance."

Chloe sipped her tea, letting the concept sink in. "That's the Bosu Ball concept," she said. "Capture the attention of each person in the audience right in the beginning by knocking them slightly off balance by saying something they don't expect, making a provocative statement or challenge a way of thinking. It will be different for every audience and situation, but you'll be able to figure out a good way to create the paradigm shift as you prepare for each presentation. Sometimes, I don't figure it out until hours or minutes before I give the presentation."

Mack broke in, "The important part is being sure they have the new balance or a new way of thinking about something, which is a part of that filling up the emotional fuel tank you explained to me early on."

"Exactly," Chloe said. "You're giving people a reason to hear you out. You're sparking a curiosity. You're creating interest. Reason, curiosity, and interest are powerful emotional motivators."

Each took another drink of tea. Chloe glanced up at the wall to check the time on the wall clock behind Mack. She said, "Listen, my class starts up in five minutes. You're welcome to join me if you want." She smiled a wry grin.

"I really appreciate the offer," Mack said with a cheesy smile. "But, I have a root canal scheduled with my dentist that I don't want to miss."

The two laughed briefly. "Okay," Chloe said. "I know you have a big speech at your annual shareholders' meeting in a few weeks. You've made some great progress. I have one more of these exercises. We need to grab lunch downtown in about a week. I'll set it up through Mary."

BULLET POINTS

Poor presentations condition people to expect poor presentations. You have only moments to capture the audience and prove the stereotypes wrong. The Bosu Ball analogy is really about creating a bit of a surprise factor. You've been in an audience enough to know the low level of expectation so many of us have when hearing someone speak for the first time. Why would people in your audience be any different? (Hint: they're not any different.)

At one point in my circuitous career path, I was a television news director at a small market station. A constant stream of résumés and videotapes came across my desk from people fresh out of school, desperately searching for the first job. The videotapes contained stories the applicants had created for a campus TV production while in college or possibly while interning at a real TV station. I could spot a viable candidate within five seconds of pushing play. Ask most news directors, and they'll share a similar story. You're the same way. Oh, yes, *you*. You are the same way. Think about it. You constantly make snap decisions about what you like. How can you possibly flip through hundreds of TV stations in search of something to watch, spending mere moments on each channel waiting for something to catch your eye?

Culture conditions us to make snap decisions, expect instant gratification, and experience immediate responses. We're talking about the microwave generation. Research website analytics and you'll see what I'm writing about. The web page has to capture and hold your attention. The web page developer doesn't have ninety seconds to grab your attention. The web developer has a fleeting moment. Since culture is conditioned to quick judgment calls, interactions, and responses, you must realize you can't change the culture. You must adapt to it as a presenter.

Bullet Point 17: Quickly knocking each audience member off the proverbial Bosu Ball, which means quickly catching them and bringing them to a new sense of balance paradigm, is one of the quickest ways to shatter expectations, connect with people, and start filling emotional fuel tanks.

Why do you think I started the fable in this book with the words, "A small bead of sweat began to form . . . ?" Because you most likely picked up this book expecting just another prescriptive approach to increasing presentation effectiveness. I had to knock you off balance and change your paradigm. Hopefully, by this time in the story, you are experiencing a new paradigm in the way you think about presenting.

ACTION

- Watch how expert presenters employ the Bosu Ball principle. You'll see the pros use a variety of ways to capture audience attention within the first moments of a presentation.

One of the quickest ways to lose an audience is to start a presentation with a canned (and often disingenuous) opening statement. How many presenters have you experienced who start with a monotone voice and deadpan look, "I'm so excited to be here with you today. Thank you to the organizers for allowing me to tell you about . . ." Then, it gets worse. "I'd like to talk to you about . . . blah, blah, blah." What do you do when someone starts a presentation like that? Tune out? Hmmm. Why would it be any different for people in your audience?

Bullet Point 18: If you start your presentation like every other boring, disengaging presentation you've heard, the audience reaction and outcome will be the same. You must be you and you must be different from the others.

I've found the best ways to gain attention immediately is to start a presentation by telling a very current, relevant story. I don't say hello, thank you, it's good to be here, or any other pleasantry. I start with a story. The story must be relevant and timely, preferably occurring within the past twenty-four hours.

If you need to capture the attention of a noisy audience where people are not paying attention to the stage, the best tool I've found is "Shhhhhh." Yes, just like you're shhhhh-shing a child who's being noisy. Keep the volume low and lengthen it out a bit. A wave of silence will overtake the room.

14

READING THE AUDIENCE

"Researchers have found that even more than IQ, your emotional awareness and abilities to handle feelings will determine your success and happiness in all walks of life."
—John Gottman, *Raising an Emotionally Intelligent Child*

"So, what makes you curious?" Chloe asked Mack. The two were sitting at a sidewalk table in front of a downtown restaurant. While the area was sectioned off with a low, ornate, wrought iron fence, the rest of the sidewalk was bustling with people enjoying the sunshine on the warm spring day.

"I'm curious about how things work," Mack said. "When I was a kid, I loved to tear things apart. I didn't care if it was a radio, my mom's blender, my remote control car; if I could take it apart and figure out how it worked, I'd do it. Now, putting all those things back together, that's a different story."

"Do you ever wonder what makes people tick?" Chloe asked.

"What do you mean?" Mack was getting better at responding to Chloe's questions with questions.

"Why do people behave the way they do?" Chloe nonchalantly nodded her head in the direction of a couple, holding hands, smiling, and talking to one another, nearly oblivious to their surroundings. "Take them for instance," she continued. "What's their story?"

"Wow, I've never thought about it like that," Mack said.

"I call it people watching," Chloe said. "I'll pick out a couple like that and ask, 'What's their story?'"

"So," Mack said, a hint of curiosity in his voice. "What is their story?"

"They've been married a couple of months. Everything about this married life thing is a new experience. They don't have a lot of money; they probably work in the same office building; they want some exercise on their lunch break, and they like to dream about the future."

"Okay," Mack said incredulously. "How in the world did you come up with that?"

"Easy," Chloe said. "They are obviously incredibly happy. I know they are newly married because each has a wedding ring on, they are young, and they are holding hands. Haven't you heard the term, wedded bliss? The looks on their faces say bliss."

Chloe paused to look at the couple who was now disappearing into the crowd. "Neither carried a bag, and she was holding an ice cream cone. Did you notice her share a bite with him? Money is tight, so they bought a single ice cream to share. They were each wearing walking shoes. If she were in downtown to impress, she would not be wearing comfortable walking shoes."

"Are you some kind of a detective?" Mack asked, almost with an air of seriousness in his voice.

"Mack," Chloe looked at him. "If you're serious about sharpening your presentation skills, you need to hone your people skills. Remember, it's audience first, whether it's an audience of one person, ten, one hundred, or one thousand people. Watching for cues is the best way to read an audience. And just like everything else we've discovered through this process, practice is required."

"It's one thing to pick two people out of a crowd and make a guess about their story," Mack said. "But how do you do that when you're presenting?"

Chloe said, "It starts before you present by creating a composite of your audience in your head. Think about the experiences so many people have before taking a seat at the boardroom table or in an auditorium. Each person arrives with a story, a background, emotional baggage, and preoccupying thoughts. What are those things we all have in common?"

Chloe could tell Mack was still having a tough time grasping the concept. "Here's a technique I use," she said. "Imagine running into a complete stranger in the produce aisle of the grocery store. Out of the blue, that person stops you and just happens to ask you a specific question about the presentation you have to give. When I say create a composite, make that person the composite of people who will be in your audience. What's the average age? Male or female? What's the time of day? If it's morning, they've just experienced the morning commute, getting the kids to school, and whatever else goes into getting to work in the morning. Is it middle of the afternoon? After a big lunch? You need to take into account all these environmental factors when thinking about the composite of your audience."

"Ahhh," Mack said with a smile. "Radio station WIIFM: what's in it for me."

Chloe said, "That's it. Reading the audience starts before the presentation. It's so important to remember, I'm finding as many ways as possible to drive home the point."

"You still haven't answered my question about reading the audience during the presentation," Mack said.

"It will come with practice, as you read people in other settings. Reading the audience while you speak will be easier when you have a level of confidence in being genuine, authentic, and vulnerable, truly caring about people. You'll watch for a number of people fidgeting, checking cell phones, or dozing off. You'll see confused looks."

"So, we sit toward the back of the sanctuary at our church," Mack said, interrupting Chloe. "An older gentleman sits near us and halfway through the service, like clockwork, he falls asleep. I always wonder how the pastor doesn't let that distract him."

"Your pastor realizes what every seasoned presenter knows," Chloe paused for effect. "There will be a sleeper, an angry person, a distracted person, an iPhone worshiper, in every audience."

"An iPhone worshiper?" Mack asked. "What's that?"

"It's the person who has their head down like they're praying, but you can see the blue glow of the phone screen on their face. Nothing you or any seasoned presenter does can pull them away from the screen. Don't worry about 'em," Chloe said with a wave of her hand.

Both Mack and Chloe took a moment to look at people walking by.

"You're looking for constant patterns," Chloe said. "When you're tuned into your audience, you'll see those individuals who are sleeping or whispering or whatever, ignore them. However, if several people are distracted and being a distraction, you need to act to remedy the situation."

Mack said, "And how exactly do I remedy the situation where people in the audience are losing interest?"

"Change it up," Chloe said. "If it's a meeting, stop and say, 'I may not be as clear as I should be. Do you have any questions?' If it's a crowd, walk out into the audience. Change the volume of your voice. Pause. Do whatever you need to do to break through the barriers and reengage the audience."

Mack aptly summed up the issue, "The hyperpace of 24/7 news, TVs all over the place, constant connection through tablets and smartphones and social media have really hurt our attention span."

"And it's imperative we as presenters realize the impact," Chloe said. "People consume information at a much faster pace. I figure I need to change up my presentation style every five minutes to maintain attention. I'll tell a story, show a very short video, share relevant data, change my location, turn on a screen, turn off a screen. I'm creating a specific shift every five minutes." She stopped speaking and looked out onto the sidewalk thoughtfully. "Just look at us. We're surrounded by so much stimuli. As a presenter, you can't expect people to walk into a conference room or boardroom and slam on the brakes. You, the presenter, have to facilitate the slowdown and understand the audience. Become a people watcher, Mack."

BULLET POINTS

Intent is dangerous for a presenter. If I say to myself, "I intend to win the audience over to my way of thinking" or "I'm interested in this topic, so if I'm intent on it, everyone else should be, too," I'll fail miserably. Why? Because I didn't take time to understand human nature and those around me. We judge ourselves by our intent. We judge others by their actions.

Sincere care for the audience begins before the presentation and carries through to the end—and after. Create the composite of your audience in your mind so you craft a meaningful, emotional, fuel-tank-filling experience, then watch carefully for comprehension and understanding during the presentation. If you make promises, follow up and follow through after the presentation.

The only way to get good at reading the audience is to improve your EI (emotional intelligence). EI is simply your ability to identify and assess your emotions and those of others.

TTI Success Insights (http://www.ttisuccessinsights.com) provides a strong assessment tool to measure your EI. I joke with people that I flunked the assessment the first time I took it. It opened my eyes that I was not paying close attention and being empathetic with those around me. I made a concerted effort to improve areas of empathy, understanding, and watching for cues from those around me. I took the same assessment a couple of years later and improved my EI dramatically.

Whether you take an assessment or not, get in the habit of watching for the reaction of others. Make it a habit by doing it continually.

Bullet Point 19: A thought becomes an action, an action becomes a habit, and habit becomes your character. Make a habit of identifying and assessing your emotions and the emotions of those around you.

READING THE AUDIENCE

What nonverbals are you watching for in an audience? I look for the finger tappers, iPhone prayers, and sleepers. If I see a number of people acting bored (finger tappers), I know it's time to change up the presentation. IPhone prayers are those people with heads down, looking at the smartphone screen. There will always be a few in the audience, but if a lot of people are more engaged with the phone than you, there's a problem. There might be a sleeper or two, but more than that is a signal to pay attention.

I strive to be an audience member I want to have in my audience. If I'm in the audience, I want to be the one leaning forward slightly, eyes on the presenter, a genuine smile on my face, and pen and paper in hand taking notes, not easily distracted by phones or those around me. Those are all signs of an engaged audience member.

15

THE SPEECH

"Nerves are natural. They prove you care. Don't let a few butterflies get the best of you! Channel the adrenaline and leave your worries behind."
—Lauren M. Hug, communications coach and trial attorney

Get your butterflies in formation. The five-word phrase had become a favorite for Mack. Early on in his coaching sessions with Chloe, he had asked how to get rid of butterflies. She said the butterflies should always be present. Keep the butterflies in formation. "A little stress going into a presentation will keep the presenter sharp," Chloe said.

Mack was moments away from taking the stage at the annual shareholders' meeting. Steve Prichett, InCirq's CEO, had noticed Mack's dramatic improvement in presenting to the board and with the leadership team. Steve wasn't alone. The leadership team, by unanimous vote, decided Mack should present the strategic direction for the company in the coming year.

Steve reported an overview of InCirq's financial performance, shareholder value and returns, and then paused and said, "We're changing things up a bit this year. It's important for you to know that the leadership team at InCirq is probably one of the best in the industry, definitely the best in the company's history. The talent represented on this stage is tremendous."

Mack looked out over the vast, darkened auditorium. The bright lights glaring down from high above created a white halo effect around the CEO as he stood at the podium. Mack could catch tiny dust particles floating in the stream of light. The feeling was surreal. His butterflies, while definitely present, were definitely in formation. He was breathing deeply, thinking about how he would create a memorable experience for the four hundred people sitting in the darkened room. "Fill their tanks," he thought to himself.

Mack and the twenty-four-member leadership team sat slightly behind and to the side of the podium on the expansive elevated stage.

"Mack Thompson has elevated operational efficiency at InCirq to new levels. He has a crystal clear picture of why we exist, what we do, and how we do it. After a collaborative approach to laying out the vision for InCirq in the next year, the leadership team decided, unanimously I might add, to have Mack present it to you this afternoon. Mack, show us the way into the new fiscal year."

Within the past five seconds, Mack had made his way toward the podium and was now standing next to Steve Pritchett. The two shook hands and Mack walked up to the podium, laid a single note card with three bullet points and a solitary phrase in big block letters circled at the bottom on top of the podium.

Polite applause gently echoed through the auditorium, quickly quieting.

"Would every one stand up," Mack asked, extending his arms, palms facing up, making a raising motion with his hands. Mack could hear a slight murmur in the crowd and people began to stand. "Tight competition, a tough market, and new pressures every day mean you are finding new ways to turn challenges into opportunities for InCirq. I asked you to stand because after hearing our CEO, Steve Prichett, talk about a company as financially strong as InCirq is, breaking into new markets and seizing market share, you deserve a standing ovation, and there's no one better to recognize the fifteen thousand employees of InCirq than with the board and shareholders."

Mack had never felt his voice so strong and his confidence so sure as the crowd erupted in applause. That was it. He changed the paradigm. This wasn't going to be another boring report.

As the applause quieted, the words were ready to roll off Mack's tongue. "Our vision is shaped by a clear understanding of who we are as InCirq and the values we hold dear. Let me share a story to illustrate. Her name is Abiah."

Mack shared the story of the jaded InCirq employee in Ulsoor, India, explaining her challenge of being wooed away by a competitor and the struggle she experienced in making a career decision. InCirq's core value of putting people first resolved the situation, keeping Abiah as a valuable part of the team.

"We have fifteen thousand stories of people who bring their best to InCirq each day, creating the competitive advantage making us number one in this industry."

Mack paused, looking thoughtfully across the audience. "That's why our vision for the next twelve months is an ambitious challenge to stretch us as individuals and as a corporation further than we can imagine. One thing I know, we can't be scared of the unknown."

Mack glanced down at his notes. He was on schedule and on point. "Have you heard the name Erik Weihenmayer?" Mack paused again, relying on his ears to check for understanding in the audience. The dull murmur revealed most had not heard the name.

"Erik was born with an eye disease that caused him to go completely blind by thirteen," Mack began telling the story of challenge, struggle, and resolution. "Erik loved sports. If there was a ball, a net, a goal, or a stick, he wanted to be in the middle of the action. And at thirteen, he vowed not to let his blindness define him. He refused to use a cane or learn Braille. But he quickly learned he wasn't able to play the sports he'd grown up with. So, he took up wrestling. By the end of high school, Erik went to the National Freestyle Wrestling Championships. It was said Erik could see things no one else could see because he could feel the next move of his opponent.

"After high school, Erik went on to college and climbed the highest mountains on the seven continents. There's a video of him climbing Everest where an aluminum extension ladder is laid across a crevasse that is several hundred feet deep. The ladder is a bridge. You see his heavy hiking boot with steal claws take that first timid step onto the ladder as he says," Mack looked down at his note card to be sure he got the words exactly right, "'Sometimes people assume that if you can't see how far you have to fall, you're not afraid. But I sometimes think that falling into the unknown is scarier than falling into something you can see.'

"For Erik, every step is a step into the unknown. That doesn't keep him from being a world class athlete as an acrobatic skydiver, long distance biker, marathon runner, skier, mountaineer, ice climber, and rock climber."

Mack stepped away from the podium and toward the edge of the stage, leaning forward slightly, he lowered his voice and said, "I share this story, not to be in awe of Erik, but to remind all of us that stepping into the unknown takes courage. With that level of determination, InCirq is moving ahead."

THE SPEECH

Mack could feel the crowd's energy as he paused. A hushed awe swept the room as people visualized Erik Weihenmayer and his courageous approach to life.

"Now, our mission is clear at InCirq. We produce quality memory. Thanks to people dedicated to innovation, we build quality memory at the lowest price point in the industry. Our global footprint gives us the advantage in two areas. People from diverse backgrounds with incredible talent devote their time to InCirq, and we have access to raw materials no other manufacturer can match."

Mack was vaguely aware that three video cameras were trained on him, capturing his image and words to be broadcast around the world via the video app he had been instrumental in developing. Many of InCirq's fifteen thousand employees were watching (and cheering) as Mack delivered the presentation. People weren't only cheering for the message but for the messenger. Most had sat with Mack in conference and break rooms at InCirq offices around the globe as he made his way on a listening tour within the past couple years. They were having a hard time believing this was the same person who seemed so uncomfortable in front of small groups. Mack owned the stage and his confidence was visible through the camera.

"InCirq will stay true to its mission and focus on growing success in three ways," Mack said, holding up his right hand, displaying three extended fingers. "First, everyone gets heard. We have access to the top talent in the memory industry. From the intern to the seasoned engineer, each and every person has an idea. We're looking for ways to take those ideas and make them reality, finding new efficiencies and market opportunities.

"Mike was heard," Mack said. "Mike is an engineer in one of our R & D labs. Mike was trying to find new uses for one of InCirq's proprietary chips. He paired our chip with a prototype miniaturized HD camera chip from one of our partners. But Mike thought he had a challenge on his hands. He was not sure his discovery was within the scope of his job or what we are trying to accomplish at InCirq. It's a lot like the invention of the sticky note. The inventor at first thought he had failed at making a new adhesive because it wasn't sticky enough, and he actually spawned a multibillion-dollar product line.

"Mike may be onto something similar. He showed me and his team what he had discovered with the InCirq chip and camera, and in doing so, activated the second key to our success; we have a commitment to learning. We're learning new app-building techniques. We're learning about new collaborative tools. We're learning what our customers want. Well, Mike quickly learned that he could tap into a team of app developers within InCirq to make full use of the technology he discovered, simply by continually seeking to learn. Think about the power of the inquisitive mind.

"And that leads us to the third key to success. Remember, I said Mike was a little nervous about revealing his discovery. He feared failure, which is perfectly natural. However, fear is not a part of our success. Failure is acceptable as long we embrace the idea that we will fail fast. We will be the new-idea company in the coming year. People will be encouraged to innovate new ideas, new processes, and new systems. They'll make educated small bets because we're constantly learning and we're ready to accept the fact that not every idea will work. We'll test it and move forward. We see company after company embrace these principles with tremendous success. The three keys are our keys—and part of our vision—for InCirq's success in the coming year."

Mack paused, thinking it was time to check the audience for understanding. The large auditorium was silent. Mack could feel his heartbeat. Only this time it wasn't the fear of presenting. "No, this time my butterflies are in formation," he thought to himself. He could sense rapt attention from those sitting in front of him.

THE SPEECH

Mack began wrapping up his presentation, purposefully walking across the stage, looking intently into the audience. "In conclusion, if you're a stockholder or board member, you see InCirq is in capable hands. If you're an employee, you are the reason for our current level of success. We're focused on our reason for existence with renewed strength and determination. We stand ready to seize opportunities. We are not promising perfection; we will make mistakes. Yet with clarity of purpose, an ear tuned to top talent, and a focus on learning, we see a clear path to growing our dominance in the international memory industry. This is our year."

The crowd erupted in applause.

BULLET POINTS

You can do it. Get out of your head. Presenting isn't about you and your nerves. Presenting is about adding value, inspiring action, and being your real, authentic, genuine self.

Realize you communicate far more than you think. Treat each and every communication as an opportunity to hone your listening and speaking skills. Be ready to communicate effectively each time you have the chance to share information.

Most of all, have fun being a powerful presenter.

Bullet Point 20: Enjoy the opportunity to share your thoughts and knowledge—all with the sincere desire to help those in the audience.

EPILOGUE

After a long, energetic round of applause, Mack took his seat at the table of other executives. His presentation had been held for the end of the meeting. Steve Prichett made a few closing remarks and called the meeting to a close.

As the house lights came on, the executives stood and immediately crowded in around Mack, offering words of congratulations. "Thank you. It was an honor," was about all Mack could say as people talked about his performance.

Then, out of the corner of his eye, Mack caught a glimpse of two women standing in the shadows next to the stairs that led from the stage to the floor of the auditorium. It was Ellie and Chloe, standing next to one another, trying to contain their excitement.

Mack excused himself from the group with another round of thank yous. He nearly jogged down the stairs, arriving at the base and taking Ellie in his arms. "Oh, Mack," she said, emotion welling in her voice. "You did it. I knew it was always inside of you. Now everyone knows as well. That was fantastic."

As the two stepped away from their embrace, Mack turned to Chloe, shaking his head, trying to clear his head from the excitement. "Wow, Chloe," Mack said. "I couldn't have done it without you. Thank you so much."

"Mack," Chloe said. "That was impressive. You're going on the speaking circuit after a performance like that."

"Let's go grab a bite to eat," Mack said as the two women turned to walk with him, one on either side. He put an arm around the shoulder of each and said, "Chloe, can you join us?"

"Sure," Chloe said. "Sounds good."

"By the way," Mack said as the three walked up the steeply inclined aisle toward the back of the auditorium. "I owe you a conversation about partnership opportunities with InCirq. Isn't that where this adventure in learning how to present started?"

Chloe leaned in to Mack, laughed, and said, "I thought you'd never ask."

RESOURCES:

BULLET POINTS

1. Be aware of your surroundings and the people around you.

2. A strong relationship at home is an important piece in the puzzle that makes up a strong, confident presenter.

3. Don't be scared to ask for help. Thinking that you know it all or being too fearful to seek a coach is a dangerous frame of mind.

4. Remind yourself that most people *want* to see you present well.

5. Embrace the paradigm shift. Your presentation isn't about you; it's about the audience. Are you more in love with the topic than the people are? If so, change your priorities.

6. Reading builds your vocabulary and communication skills. Be a voracious reader.

7. Connect the confidence you have in your knowledge and the confidence you have in communicating on an interpersonal level with family, friends, and coworkers.

8. As human beings, our minds are wired to learn from and respond to stories. If you want the information you present to be memorable, tell a story.

9. Being a good communicator is rooted in servant leadership.

10. Do your homework. People know you care by your actions and the amount of time you invest in getting to know those with whom you are communicating.

11. As you create the road map (outline, text, bullet points, etc.) for your presentation, stay focused on the destination. Be dedicated.

12. Preparation lays a foundation for success.

13. The meeting before the meeting is an effective way to think about your audience first. You're preparing, connecting ahead of time, seeking clarity, and paving the way for effective, efficient communication.

14. Three steps to crisis communication: (1) own it, (2) fix it, and (3) prevent it from happening again.

15. Great stories have three things in common: challenge, struggle, and resolution (CSR).

16. Share your knowledge with others.

17. Quickly knocking each audience member off the proverbial Bosu Ball, which means quickly catching them and bringing them to a new sense of balance paradigm, is one of the quickest ways to shatter expectations, connect with people, and start filling emotional fuel tanks.

18. If you start your presentation like every other boring, disengaging presentation you've heard, the audience reaction

and outcome will be the same. You must be you and you must be different from the others.

19. A thought becomes an action, an action becomes a habit, and habit becomes your character. Make a habit of identifying and assessing your emotions and the emotions of those around you.

20. Enjoy the opportunity to share your thoughts and knowledge—all with the sincere desire to help those in the audience.

RESOURCES:

SEVEN LAWS OF PRESENTING

1. Character counts.

What you do in private matters and someday, somehow, some-where, will be revealed in public.

2. Be real, authentic, and genuine.

It's redundant for a reason. Being yourself is critical to your success. People have a tuned-in "fake" meter. Set that meter off, and you lose the audience.

3. Seek wisdom.

Continually growing your knowledge and putting it into practice will build skills and grow talents.

4. Tell stories.

Stories are memorable and will make the information you share in a presentation memorable. Illustrate every point you want to make with a story.

5.   Audience first.

Period.

6.   Start with the end in mind.

Accomplish just one thing with each presentation and do it well by staying focused on the destination.

7.   Be grateful.

An attitude of genuine gratitude is appealing. Thankfulness is attractive. Wear it often.

ACKNOWLEDGMENTS

To every person who invited me to speak to a group, thank you. Each presentation opportunity has taught me something new. To my clients who invite me into their lives and businesses, I am most grateful for the chance to learn ways to help you achieve the potential inside of you.

Much of what is written on these pages comes directly from the lessons that I learned from presenting more than fifty times a year and coaching many people on tapping into the gift of communication that resides in each one of us.

Daily, I consider the richest blessing in my life: that of my parents, Dan and Bonnie. Thank you for instilling a work ethic in me, praying me through those challenging teenage years, and for consistently setting an example of true character, integrity, generosity, love, and humility.

Dale Peterson, you gave me an open microphone and transmitter. Thank you for entrusting the keys of a radio station to a sixteen-year-old kid. Even if it was 6:00 a.m. on a Sunday morning, the lessons learned through your phone calls immediately after that first newscast of the morning helped shape me into the communicator I am today.

Joe Martin, you've opened the TV news door to so many young people. I'm grateful to be one of those fortunate to sit in front of the camera for you.

Ron Price, Brandon Wright, and Brice Sloan, thank you for friendship and encouragement. Iron sharpens iron. I appreciate your honesty, innovative approach, and leadership.

Isn't it amazing how a few words can be so difficult? Thank you Justin Foster for leading us out of the maze of a subtitle and into the simplicity of saying exactly what the book is about: A Story About Overcoming the Fear of Public Speaking.

I opened the door through LinkedIn, asking people to review the Sweating Bullets manuscript. I'm incredibly grateful and indebted to the following people for accepting the challenge, reading the manuscript, and providing insightful feedback to make this book what it is today (in no particular order): Brice Sloan, Brandon Wright, Christy Stansell, Brenda Maynard, John Riggins, Dr. Marilyn Martin Melchiorre, Holly Beech, Dr. Ken Swaim, Dan Whiting, Bryan Taylor, Donna Shines, Tracy L. Basterrechea, Carl Wilgus, and Stacy McNeill.

A special thank you to Maryanna Young and your team at Aloha Publishing. Your encouragement, prodding, and whip cracking were more necessary than you know. Kim Foster, you did a fabulous job as editor, and I so appreciate your approach to clarity and strengthening the intent of each word. Cari Campbell, I marvel at your creativity and am grateful that you are able to put the noise and clutter of competing ideas aside to do masterful work in cover design.

Tonia, Jordan, and Chloe, my family. Thank you. Thank you for your patience through this process. Most of all, thank you for your love.

ACKNOWLEDGMENTS

No acknowledgment would ever do justice to my love and admiration for each of you.

My Lord and Savior, Jesus Christ. Thank you for Your incredible gifts. May I be a true disciple and simply a reflection of You.

THANK YOU!

I sincerely thank you for reading Sweating Bullets. My only desire is that it help you be the communicator you were created to be.

I do have a couple favors to ask.

First, would you send me an email? I'd love to hear what you thought of the book or you can simply say, hi. Send the message to info@daledixonmedia.com.

Second, would you write a review of the book on Amazon? Go to amazon.com, search for Sweating Bullets in the book section and follow the instructions for leaving a review. It's a big help in fulfilling my mission of helping people be better communicators through this book. More reviews results in a higher ranking, which results in more people having the opportunity to buy the book.

ALSO FROM DALE DIXON:

Thrive, Leap the Threshold from Survival to Success
(Early 2014 Release)

FIND DALE AT:

Web: daledixonmedia.com
E-mail: info@daledixonmedia.com
Twitter: @ddixonmedia
Facebook: http://facebook.com/dale.dixon
LinkedIn: http://www.linkedin.com/pub/dale-dixon/8/153/698

DALE CAN CUSTOM-TAILOR THE FOLLOWING KEYNOTE ADDRESSES TO YOUR GROUP:

Face the Fear to Thrive
Attitude Determines Altitude
Get Rid of Your Dinosaur Gene
Influence Change
Communicate through Earned Media
Powerful Presentations
Just Because It's Legal Doesn't Make It Right

ABOUT THE AUTHOR

Dale Dixon is founder of Dale Dixon Media, dedicated to helping people fulfill their potential in effectively communicating a message. Dale specializes in improving on-camera and presentation performance.

Dale is also President and CEO of the Better Business Bureau, serving the Snake River Region. The private, nonprofit organization helps companies to sell ethically and people to buy wisely. In that role, he presents more than fifty times per year and is the subject of hundreds of interviews with print, TV, and radio journalists annually.

At the age of sixteen, Dale was provided his first opportunity to "present." As a junior in high school, he started a broadcast news career at a radio station. The chance to tell stories into a microphone turned into a passion that led Dale into the TV news business.

In total, Dale spent fourteen years in the broadcast news business, working as a reporter, morning anchor, evening anchor, and news director for CBS, ABC, and NBC affiliates in local markets.

Working in television news often means uprooting one's family and moving to a bigger city every few years. While Dale enjoyed the work, he knew the lifestyle was not what he wanted while starting and raising a family. He was offered and accepted a position as a public information officer in Idaho's second largest city. Since that time, Dale has stayed engaged with news media in addition to coaching and teaching communication strategy from the classroom to the C-suite.

Dale lives in Meridian, Idaho, with his wife, Tonia and their two children.

DALE ALSO RECOMMENDS:

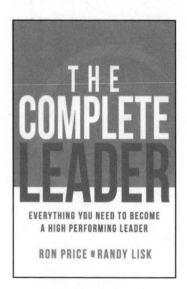

THE COMPLETE LEADER
Ron Price & Randy Lisk

As executive coaches, the authors have combined experience and tools gleaned from decades working with leaders from Fortune 100 companies to small businesses. The result is a book that outlines the skills and abilities necessary for leadership excellence in a customizable and scaleable format.

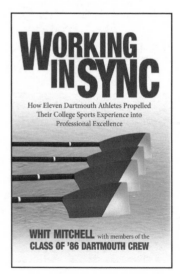

WORKING IN SYNC
Whit Mitchell

Eleven highly successful professionals learned the principles of connection and teamwork on the Dartmouth Class of '86 crew. Years later, the lessons have had a profound impact on their lives and the lives of those around them. Meet the crew whose stories will change everything about the way you do business and lead your team.